T0367929

神道 祝詞
SHINTO NORITO
A BOOK OF PRAYERS

IN THE TRADITION OF
TSUBAKI GRAND SHRINE
椿大神社

Ann Llewellyn Evans

Foreword by Yukitaka Yamamoto

Trafford rev. 08/24/2018

 www.trafford.com

North America & international
toll-free: 1 888 232 4444 (USA & Canada)
fax: 812 355 4082

DEDICATED TO

Guji Yukitaka Yamamoto

A remarkable man who
shines with the light of the kami

御神光を受け
燦然と輝く偉大なる

山本行隆宮司に捧ぐ

CONTENTS

神道 祝詞
SHINTO NORITO
A BOOK OF PRAYERS

FOREWORD

Shinto is the way of living with Great Nature and therefore is positive and simple. Rather than focusing on theology and doctrine, Shinto centers on *jissen* 実践, or practice. As a result, we find that the practice of Shinto leads us to live in harmony with *Dai Shizen no meguri* 大自然の巡り, the ceaseless cycle of Great Nature.

In Shinto, all human beings are regarded as children or descendants of the kami 神. Therefore, we have kami nature 神性 within ourselves and are born with the capability of solving problems and of creating a life with happiness and peace for others as well as ourselves.

Because we are children of the kami, we have the ability to get closer to the kami. Although we may become distant by not following the proper path, through purification we are able to renew ourselves, to cultivate our spirituality, *reisei* 霊性, and to restore our original kami nature.

In my shrine, Tsubaki Ō Kami Yashiro, we practice waterfall purification, *misogi* 禊, throughout the year. In the severe winter season, it is indeed a challenge to be exposed to below-zero temperatures while standing under an icy waterfall. This ancient ritual of physical and spiritual cleansing is a means for us to correct our path and to become one with Great Nature and the kami.

In daily life, Shinto practice is deeply embedded. People wash their faces and bodies first thing in the morning after rising. Then we face and pray to the sun and to the kami enshrined in the home shrine, the *kamidana* 神棚, after dedicating the offerings of washed rice, natural salt, and water. At the end of each day, we pray once again to the kami to express our appreciation, *kansha* 感謝, for being able to live, eat, work and to complete the day without problems. This continuous practice goes throughout the year and even through our lifetimes.

Shinto is the practice of personal improvement, of correcting one's path; this attitude and practice builds strength in character and in spirit. We become more appreciative and enjoy working and helping other people with a positive attitude toward life.

In Shinto each individual stands on a vertical line connecting the kami, your ancestors and your descendants, past and future. Additionally, each person is also on a horizontal line that connects you with your neighbor, your friends, society, country, and with foreign nations.

In the vertical line, *tate no musubi* 縦の結び, we respect and revere our ancestors and the kami, *keishin suso* 敬神崇祖, as well as respecting and honouring our descendants. In the horizontal line, we respect and harmonize with other people, *kyōzon kyōei* 共存共栄, in our local as well as in our world communities. Shinto calls this *kannagara* 惟神.

Through constant practice of purification, by correcting our paths (*harai kiyome* 祓い清め) through *misogi* 禊, the crosspoint of the vertical and horizontal lines where we as human beings reside will be lifted closer to the kami. By steady practice, we see the kami beyond our ancestors in our vertical connection, *tate no musubi* 縦の結び, and we obtain the strength to work for the benefit of other people across the horizontal connection, *yoko no musubi* 横の結び.

Although Shinto is regarded as the indigenous religion of Japan, the precepts and practices of Shinto can be understood and meaningful to people throughout the world. Spirituality is a basis for sharing among all races, all nationalities. It is my strong belief that this *kannagara*, the Shinto way of spirituality, can be shared and understood by people other than Japanese and that Shinto can contribute toward peace in the world.

There are few books about Shinto available in English. Most books that are available in English discuss Shinto from an academic approach. This Norito book by Rev. Ann Evans focuses on the practice of Shinto. Shinto "cannot be taught but must be caught"; it must be experienced, not learned. Thus, this book is most important as the first book in history that is written about Shinto, in English, from the viewpoint of a practitioner.

Rev. Evans has visited Tsubaki Grand Shrine for many years. Each time she visited, she spent at least a week there and practiced *misogi* at the Konryu Myojin Waterfall every day. I must say that she experienced and learned deeply about Tsubaki Shingaku, the teaching of Tsubaki, the essence of Kannagara no Michi.

Rev. Evans conducts Shinto ceremonies daily and practices *misogi* regularly. She was ordained as a Shinto priestess after going through long and intensive training. Therefore, this book is not written by a person investigating Shinto, but by a person of true spiritual commitment to Shinto.

This book is extremely important and unique. It provides the readers with a method to pronounce the Norito in Japanese. This is very important, since the Japanese language has a spiritual meaning in its pronunciation, intonation and in the kanji themselves; we refer to this deeper, multi-level meaning as *kotodama* 言霊 "spirit of the word." I appreciate Rev. Evans' courage and tremendous effort to introduce *kotodama* in this book, since no one has ever tried to deal with it in this way due to its complexity.

It is commendable that Rev. Evans translated so many Shinto Norito into English and made interpretations of them poetically, since Norito are all written in Japanese classical style, making it difficult to understand the words and sentences of such old-style language. However, Rev. Evans has successfully met the challenges of language and, through this interpretation, has more correctly conveyed the true meaning of these Norito than would be conveyed from word-to-word translation.

I totally support this poetic approach. This book is far more effective to understand the kami than dozens of other academic Shinto books. I encourage you to chant the Norito regularly so that you will sense the meaning of the prayers and that you may feel and hear the voice of the kami from this book of Norito.

Rev. Dr. Yukitaka Yamamoto
The 96th HighPriest
Tsubaki Ō Kami Yashiro
Suzuka, Mie Prefecture, Japan

INTRODUCTION

Shinto is a spiritual tradition that emphasizes each person's sacred nature. Mankind is a descendant of the kami, the spiritual beings who have existed since the universe congealed. As descendants of the kami, we have innate brightness within us. From time to time, this luster may be dulled through impurities and incorrect action. However, through the rituals of Shinto we may purify ourselves, restoring the original luster and luminosity and finding great joy in our lives.

The very simplicity of Shinto forces us to profoundly search our own hearts for the correct path, for Shinto does not provide us doctrines by which to live. Instead, it connects us to an ancient, archetypal spirituality which was developed thousands of years ago yet has permitted individual creativity and interpretation so that it remains meaningful and emotionally powerful in our modern day world.

Shinto is indigenous to Japan. However, its simple yet profound teachings apply to all humanity. Shinto is now reaching the West where we can find renewal and joy in its simple teachings.

About this book

This book presents Shinto prayers, or Norito, in a format where the English-speaking reader can both pronounce it in Japanese and can understand its meaning in English. Although this introduction will provide a brief overview of Shinto spirituality, the primary function of the book is mainly as a tool for Shinto practice and recitation of prayers.

The western practitioner of Shinto has, to date, been challenged by the limited number of books on Shinto from a spiritual perspective and has been required to learn to read Japanese writing (*hiragana*) in order to recite the Norito prayers. This has been a daunting task for many, creating an unnecessary obstacle for fully participating in and experiencing Shinto spirituality.

The prayers in this book are presented in the original Japanese *kanji*, but also in *romaji* so that the western reader may recite the prayers in the original language of classical Japanese. Because of the unique aspects of *kotodama* (explained below in this chapter), recitation should be done in the original language of Japanese rather than in English.

At first a westerner who does not speak Japanese may find the challenge of reciting prayer in a foreign language overwhelming. However, pronunciation is actually fairly simple since it is written in *romaji* in the same way it is pronounced. (See Appendix A)

The English translation and interpretation of each prayer is presented so that the non-Japanese speaking reader may understand the content and flow of the prayer. Translation of the ancient Norito is a challenging task, and I humbly ask the readers' forgiveness for any interpretations which may be inadequate or not give enough weight to the sanctity of the prayers themselves.

The language of the prayers is ancient classical Japanese and is difficult and complex, even for the best of scholars. Donald Philippi, a highly regarded translator of ancient Japanese, describes the complexity of the language of Norito:

> [They] are cast in antique language of the most flowery sort. Sentences are long and loosely-connected; the grammatical relationship of parts is difficult to determine; the meaning of many words is unclear; and everywhere semantic clarity is sacrificed to sonority.[1]

Although this imprecise use of language frustrates a clear translation, it leaves the prayer open to interpretation by each individual. Thus, an ancient tradition can also be seen through the eyes of modern man, allowing the imagery and symbols of ancient man's primordial spiritual practice to touch us in current times. The interpretation of the ancient classical form of Japanese Norito has limitless variations, even by the Japanese.

As a result, the translations and interpretations presented in this book are not precise, literal renderings favoured by academics; rather, they have been translated with poetic license to retain the poetic flow and heartfelt emotion that is such an archetypal characteristic of Norito.

Let the imagery seep into your spirit; let the sonorous sound of the kotodama, the chanting in Japanese, touch the centre of your being. The Norito and the ritual will nourish your spirituality.

Basics of Shinto

Shinto is based on spontaneous awareness of the Divine in all of creation—including mankind, other sentient beings, living nature such as trees, and natural matter such as mountains, rivers, and other formations.

"Shinto" literally is comprised of two kanji: 神, pronounced *shin* or *kami* and meaning deity, and 道, pronounced *to* or *michi* and meaning way, road, or path. Thus, *Shinto* literally means "the way of the kami," or the path of the divine; it is also commonly read as *kami no michi* which also means the "way or path of the kami."

Kami are the spiritual beings who are central to Shinto. Although some authors translate *kami* as "gods," this tends to be misleading since the western notion of "god" indicates an omnipotent being who has control over our destinies. Since the term "kami" cannot be translated appropriately into an English word, in this text the word will not be italicized as a foreign word.

The kami are a myriad of spiritual beings, more akin to the western concept of angels. These spiritual beings, or kami, have existed since the beginning of creation. As the universe congealed and took form, various spiritual beings came into being. Over time, as the universe further developed and the Earth was formed, mankind came into being as descendants of the kami. Thus we, as humans, have within us the primordial kami nature, although we are confronted by innumerable challenges throughout our human existence. Thus, we turn to spiritual beings for inspiration, guidance, and protection. In Shinto, these spiritual beings are called kami.

There is a loose hierarchy of kami just as there is of angels: *amatsu kami*, Heavenly Kami; *kunitsu kami*, Earthly Kami; and *yaoyorozu no kami*, the myriad of kami who perform additional tasks and serve broad purposes.

Since human beings are descendants of the kami, the kami are our ancestral spiritual deities. Thus, we as humans have inherited the same divinity within us; we are innately as pure and bright as our ancestral kami.

However, we develop, acquire, and commit various impurities (*tsumi* or *kegare*) through our own actions, through actions that happen to or upon us, or through being in a situation or place with negative energy. It is important that the concept of *tsumi* or *kegare* differs from that of "sin."

The western notion of sin has a judgmental connotation, whereas *tsumi* is not a judgment of iniquity, but a negative or impure blockage to the divine present within each one of us and abundant throughout all creation. More specifically, "*kegare*" describes an impure condition or state of an individual (either of one's self or of others). "*Tsumi*," on the other hand, refers to impurities that exist in relationship between two persons or groups. *Tsumi* are actions or disorders that occur or exist between one's self and other people or between one's self and nature.

Shinto practice, then, centers on sweeping away the impurities by purification of our selves and of our surroundings in order to remove obstacles and to correct our path, returning to our natural purity and radiance.

Purification of our self and of our environment enhances our sense of internal radiance; purification of our community and our world enhances cooperation, tolerance, and peace.

Shinto has no doctrine that dictates specifically how this should be done or under what rules we should live our lives. Neither is there a central figure or founder who has imparted teachings to serve as the basis for the religion. Instead, through the rituals and prayers one must use introspection and intuition to discover the true path. This requirement of the practitioner to be a central part of the discovery and the process makes the wisdom achieved more clear and more internal, rather than followers receiving a pre-defined teaching.

Shinto's scripture is Nature. The original Shinto shrines were sacred groves of trees. An area was purified, and through ritual chanting the kami were entreated to descend to the sacred site, alighting on the tops of the trees and creating a connection between Heaven and Earth, between sacred and temporal. Even for us, as modern mankind, the experience of being in an old growth forest or by a pristine, pounding waterfall, can certainly invoke awareness of the sacred.

In Shinto this awareness of Great Nature, *Dai Shizen*, is central to mankind's understanding of his relationship to the rest of creation. Great Nature goes beyond nature as trees, rivers, and living beings; it encompasses all of creation, including living nature as well as matter such as rocks, mountains, and natural formations. "In Shinto there is no separation between the universe and divine creative spirit. The universe is divine creative spirit extending itself as matter and as life." [2]

A follower of Shinto, then, acknowledges the sacredness of all creation and attempts to live a life that confirms and enhances this divinity within himself as well as in his community and environment. A commitment to the Shinto path does not exclude other spiritual beliefs, nor does it conflict or oppose other spiritual traditions. For example, a Shintoist may, and often does, practice Buddhism as well.

The way of Shinto is the path of the kami; it is an acknowledgement of divinity throughout our world and a personal commitment to live one's life with the spirituality and brightness of the original kami of creation.

Kotodama

Part of the mysticism of Shinto ritual is the vibratory connection to the divine. The importance of this vibration is experienced in the great drums (*taiko*) as well as in the manner of chanting by the priests. Each word of the Norito has significance in its sound, as well as in its meaning. This concept is called "*kotodama.*"

Kotodama is literally translated as "word soul." This attribute of the Japanese language does not transfer into English. Words have different vibratory rhythms, and thus the significance of the sound can be as important as the meaning of the word itself. For example, the kanji 神 is usually pronounced either *kami* or *shin* (as in *Shinto*). However, when the divine energy of the kami enters into a human being, the pronunciation is made more resonant, changing from *shin* to *jin*, although the kanji does not change. This reflects an actual vibratory change in the experience of divinity. Thus, using English as the language for recitation would remove many of the subtleties of the prayer itself.

Guji Yukitaka Yamamoto explains kotodama and prayer:

> When chanting, tune your vibration to the divine way. In this manner, you will hear the voice of the kamisama and you can transmit your thoughts to the kamisama. In this way, you unite with the kami. You know the kami, and the kami know you. You will understand nature and coexistence.
>
> Shinto is very simple—you are living now. You should appreciate your life. You are sustained by the kami. Be appreciative and live with gratitude. When you really feel this, and you vibrate the words of your prayers, the kami will see you and you will have infinite power, courage, and strength. You will be filled with *ki* from Heaven.[3]

The sound or rhythm of the prayer is an individual matter. Prayers should be recited from the heart and as such will have an aspect of gratitude, respect, and humility. Chant the words, finding a resonance in your own voice and style that creates a connection to the Divine. Finding and developing this vibration will be part of the process of your prayer practice.

Norito and Ritual

Shinto prayer and ritual center on recognition of the divine and on the concept of purification. Before approaching a shrine, for example, a follower rinses his hands and mouth in order to purify the physical body. Indeed, the ritual practice of *misogi*, or bathing in cold, moving water, is performed to purify one's physical body as well as one's spirit. For further discussion on *misogi*, see Appendix E.

Prayers are referred to as "*Norito*" as well as "*haishi*." Norito are more formal prayers than *haishi*. Each prayer, however, has certain common components:

- Recognition of the divine kami
- Statement of humility and gratitude
- Statement of petition or request
- Closing with reverence and humility

The purpose of ritual is to reinsert ourselves into a divine state of being, not as a new position but as an acknowledgement and reinforcement of what already exists. Ritual restores sensitive awareness to our relationship to the universe. Through purification and removal of impurities and blockages, we return to our innate internal brightness and cultivate a demeanor of gratitude and joy.

Shinto rituals and prayers were created by ancient man over 2,000 years ago, in a time when mankind was more intuitive about his relationship to his world. Because of this, the rites are archetypal and invoke deep emotion within the participants.

The rituals and the prayers of Shinto are poetry. They not only express a view of life and spirituality, they are a process through which we can touch the spiritual vibrations of life. And, like a poem, they are best not dissected in an analytical study.

The ritual of Shinto should be experienced, not analyzed—let the emotion and feeling of the ceremony wash over you as a river washes over and polishes the rocks of its riverbed. Become part of the process, and you will be fulfilled by the spiritual connections that transpire.

Ritual is formed from intuition. It is created from a sense deep within us that creates a ceremony wherein we are deeply moved, perhaps even inspired and aware of the mystical divine. The ritual itself, as a whole, becomes the experience. We may not be able to explain it; indeed perhaps we should not try lest the explanation dull the luster of the communion.

Shinto ritual, in particular, consists of archetypal, ancient practice, the meaning of which even many Japanese are unable to clearly articulate. This does not, however, mean that they do not understand "the way of the kami."

Joseph Campbell recounts a story of a western man who did not understand Shinto and requested further explanation from a Shinto priest:

> "You know," he said, "I've been now to a good many ceremonies and have seen quite a number of shrines, but I don't get the ideology; I don't get your theology."
>
> The Japanese (you may know) do not like to disappoint visitors, and this gentleman, polite, apparently respecting the foreign scholar's profound question, paused as though in deep thought, and then, biting his lips, slowly shook his head. "I think we don't have ideology," he said. "We don't have theology. We dance."
>
> That, for me, was the lesson of the congress. What it told was that in Japan, in the native Shinto religion of the land, where the rites are extremely stately, musical, and imposing, no attempt has been made to reduce their "affect images" to words. They have been left to speak for themselves—as rites, as works of art—through the eyes to the listening heart. And that, I would say, is

what we, in our own religious rites, had best be doing too. Ask an artist what his picture "means," and you will not soon ask such a question again. Significant images render insights beyond speech, beyond the kinds of meaning speech defines.[4]

I first experienced Shinto ceremony when I was traveling in Japan at the age of 19. I had little knowledge of Shinto and no conscious understanding of the ceremony, but the emotional experience touched me very deeply. I can still, to this day, recall the intensity of emotion that came over me as the *mikosan* performed the sacred dance at the end of the ceremony.

Two decades later I would return to Shinto and again the spiritual experience struck a chord deep within me. In following this path I have learned that Shinto is universal—it is not merely a Japanese tradition. It is a spiritual practice that can restore fullness and radiance to any person.

Tsubaki Ō Kami Yashiro

The prayers presented in this book are in the tradition of Tsubaki Ō Kami Yashiro, near Suzuka City in Mie Prefecture, Japan. This shrine has an ancient heritage and tradition, as it is one of the oldest shrines in all of Japan.

The shrine began in 3 B.C. as "Chiwaki Ō Kami Yashiro," meaning "Shrine at the Crossroads of Heaven and Earth." In the 4th century, Emperor Nintoku had a dream while visiting the shrine that 1,000 camellias bloomed in one night. Thereafter, the shrine name was changed to Tsubaki Ō Kami Yashiro, the word *tsubaki* meaning "camellia."

Tragedy arrived in 1580 when the warlord Nobunaga attacked many shrines and temples for political control, including Tsubaki Ō Kami Yashiro where the Shinto shrines and Buddhist temples were burned and destroyed and many priests of both faiths were killed.

During the Tokugawa period (1600 to 1868), Tsubaki Ō Kami Yashiro was protected as a sanctuary.

In 1968, Yukitaka Yamamoto became Guji, or High Priest, of Tsubaki Ō Kami Yashiro. He is the 96th generation to be Guji of this shrine, which means that for many generations his forefathers have looked after and nurtured this spiritual site.

Guji Yamamoto has overseen the rebuilding of the three main sanctuaries there. Additionally, he had a vision that Shinto would be meaningful to people in the western world, and thus he has participated in many international inter-faith events hoping to bring understanding and peace among people of the world.

Guji Yamamoto has taught for decades that Shinto's truths are universal and thus may enrich the life experiences of people outside of Japan. He has participated and served as a Director of many international inter-faith organizations.

In 1987, Guji Yamamoto and his son, Gon Guji Yukiyasu Yamamoto (Assistant High Priest) established Tsubaki Grand Shrine of America in California. This began a new sharing of spirituality between east and west. And, with the traditions rooted in ancient intuition and ritual, many people have been spiritually and emotionally touched by Shinto in the western world and now practice these prayers of ancient traditions.

The primary kami enshrined at Tsubaki Ō Kami Yashiro are:

- Sarutahiko no Ō Kami, leader of all Earthly Kami and the kami of protection and guidance
- Ame no Uzume no Mikoto, kami of meditation, divine movement, and marriage; wife of Sarutahiko no Ō Kami

At Tsubaki Ō Kami Yashiro the daily ceremony of *chohai* begins with the resounding beats of the drum, or *taiko*. The participants gather (including priests, shrine employees, and laypersons) and chant together Ō Harahi no Kotoba, Declaration of Faith, and Goshu no Shinka. The vibration and rhythm of the chanting truly create a sacred atmosphere wherein the participants pray for purification of themselves, their community, and the world.

Personal Prayer

Practice and implementation of Shinto must be done with sincerity and with focus—with *makoto*. Regular prayer reinforces the natural order of things, the ceaseless movement of the universe—*kannagara*.

In a traditional Shinto home it is customary to have a *kamidana*, a small altar, where prayers are offered to open and to close each day. Creating sacred space within one's home not only serves as a reminder of our spiritual values and objectives, it also provides a focal point for solitude, meditation, and prayer. This space may be a shelf, an alcove, or a corner. Nourish your spirit here through prayer and heart-felt gratitude expressed to the kami.

This process, this daily personal ritual, cultivates *makoto*, creating a conduit for the manifestation of *kannagara* within each of us. Morihei Ueshiba, founder of Aikido, stated:

> Rise early in the morning to greet the sun. Inhale and let yourself soar to the ends of the universe; breathe out and let the cosmos inside. Next breathe up the fecundity and vibrance of the Earth. Blend the breath of Earth with your own and become the breath of life itself. Your mind and body will be gladdened, depression and heartache will dissipate and you will be filled with gratitude.[5]

Any spiritual practice must be done with regularity and with focus—hence the reference "practice." Spirituality is not developed by intellectual means any more than the body's physical condition can be toned by reading an exercise book. Prayer and ritual are spiritual exercises—they sharpen the soul to keener awareness. On some days, the practice may be difficult and tedious. And on other days, of course, the experience will be uplifting and enlightening.

Perseverance and practice with sincerity of the heart will bring a mystical, vibrant connection to the divine.

Through the traditions of Shinto, we learn that the essence of spirituality is found within one's self, since we are inextricably part of the divine. The ceremonies and prayers of Shinto are age-old mystical practices that enable us to connect and experience our spiritual life through ritual, rather than through doctrine.

Make a habit of prayer, offering your prayers with humility, gratitude, and sincerity.

Introduction Notes:

[1] Donald L. Phillippi, *Norito: A Translation of the Ancient Japanese Ritual Prayers.* (Princeton, N.J.: Princeton University Press, 1990), p. 1.

[2] J.W.T. Mason, *The Meaning of Shinto.* (Port Washington, N.Y.: Kennikat Press, 1967). p. 44.

[3] Rev. Dr. Yukitaka Yamamoto. Interview with author October 11, 2000.

[4] Joseph Campbell, *Myths to Live By* (New York: Penguin Books, 1972), p. 102.

[5] John Stevens, *The Essence of Aikido: Spiritual Teachings of Morihei Ueshiba* (Japan: Kodansha International Ltd., 1993), p. 25.

KINEN REITSU
Pray with intensity of spirit

Rev. Dr. Yukitaka Yamamoto

身滌 大祓

高天原に神留坐す　神魯伎神魯美の詔以て　皇御祖神伊邪

那岐命　筑紫の日向の橘の小戸の阿波岐原に　禊祓へ給ひ

し時に生坐る　祓戸の大神等　諸々の枉事罪穢を　祓ひ賜

Prayer for Purification through Misogi
MISOGI NO Ō HARAI

In the Expanse of High Heaven dwell the exalted kami.
Takama no Hara ni kamu zumari masu *

By command of our divine ancestral kami,
The noble male kami and the august female kami of Heaven,
Our great ancestral kami Izanagi no Mikoto performed misogi
At Ahagihara of Odo, Tachibana of Himuka, in Tsukushi of the
    Ancient Land,
Where his very being was cleansed of all impurities by many
Great Kami of Purification.
Kamurogi Kamuromi no mikoto mochite
Sume mi oya kamu Izanagi no Mikoto
Tsukushi no Himuka no Tachibana no Odo no Ahagihara ni
Misogi harae tamaishi toki ni are maseru
Haraedo no Ō Kamitachi

I humbly beseech the kami to cleanse me of all impurities
Within myself and in my relationships with others, and
Between myself and the way of Great Nature.
Moromoro no magagoto tsumi kegare o
Harai tamae kiyome tamae to
Mōsu koto no yoshi o

* When recited in a group, this line is read only by Saishu or
  Michihiko (leader)

3

等共に　聞食せと　恐み恐みも申す

へ清め賜へと　申す事の由を　天津神國津神　八百万の神

All attendant Heavenly Kami and Earthly Kami,
Each of the myriad of kami—
Hear these modest words.
Humbly, reverently, I speak this prayer.
Amatsu kami kunitsu kami
Yaoyorozu no kamitachi tomo ni
Kikoshi mese to
Kashikomi kashikomi mo maosu

大祓詞
（おほ はらへ ことば）

高天原（たかまのはら）に神留（かむづま）り坐（ま）す　皇親神漏岐（すめらがむつかむろぎ）　神漏美（かむろみ）の命（みこと）以（も）ちて　八（や）

百万神等（ほよろづのかみたち）を　神集（かむつど）へに集（つど）へ賜（たま）ひ　神議（かむはか）りに議（はか）り賜（たま）ひて　我（あ）が

皇御孫命（すめみまのみこと）は　豊葦原水穂國（とよあしはらのみづほのくに）を　安國（やすくに）と平（たひら）けく知（し）ろし食（め）せと

Great Words of Purification
Ō HARAHI NO KOTOBA

In the Expanse of High Heaven dwell the exalted kami.
By command of our divine ancestral kami,
Takama no Hara ni kamu zumari masu *
Sumeragamutsu Kamurogi
Kamuromi no Mikoto mochite

The noble male kami and the august female kami of Heaven,
The myriad of kami from throughout the Universe
Gathered and gathered.
The kami assembled and conferred
Yaoyorozu no kamitachi o
Kamu tsudoe ni tsudoe tamai
Kamu hakari ni hakari tamaite

To give direction to the Heavenly grandchild Sumemima no
 Mikoto
To make the Ancient Land of Toyoashihara no Mizuho know
 peace and tranquility.
Aga Sumemima no Mikoto wa
Toyoashihara no Mizuho no Kuni o
Yasu kuni to taira keku shiroshi meseto

* When recited in a group, this phrase is read only by Saishu

7

事依さし奉りき　此く依さし奉りし國中に　荒振る神等を

ば　神問はしに問はし賜ひ　神掃ひに掃ひ賜ひて　語問ひ

し磐根樹根　立草の片葉をも語止めて　天の磐座放ち　天

の八重雲を伊頭の千別きに千別きて　天降し依さし

Profound matters were entrusted to this great kami;
These matters of trust were to be obeyed throughout the land.
The ways of rough malevolent kami sometimes disrupted the
    natural way of harmony.
The great kami returned these araburu kamitachi to the correct
    path;
They swept away all obstacles and impurities and purified the
    Ancient Land.
Koto yosashi matsuriki
Kaku yosashi matsurishi kunuchi ni
Araburu kamitachi o ba
Kamu towashi ni towashi tamai
Kamu harahi ni harahi tamaite

Moreover, silence was brought to the very foundation of the
    majestic trees and to the standing grass,
Even casting silence down to each single leaf.
Koto toishi iwane kine
Tachi kusa no kakiha o mo koto yamete

Thereupon, from the midst of Heaven the kami descended
Through the eight-fold layers of clouds that separate Heaven
    and Earth,
Guiding the Heavenly grandchild down to the Ancient Land
Ame no iwakura hanachi
Ame no yaegumo o Izu no chiwaki ni chiwakite
Ama kudashi yosashi matsuriki

奉りき　此く依さし奉りし四方の國中と　大倭日高見國を

安國と定め奉りて　下つ磐根に宮柱太敷き立て　高天原に

千木高知りて　皇御孫命の瑞の御殿仕へ奉りて　天の御蔭

日の御蔭と隠り坐して　安國と平けく知ろし食さむ國中に

成り出でむ　天の益人等が　過ち犯しけむ種種の罪事は

10

To bring order and tranquility throughout the four directions of
the Earth.
People of the Ancient Land of Ō Yamato Hidaka Mi no Kuni
trusted and followed the way of Nature.
Harmony and peace were established throughout the Land.
Kaku yosashi matsurishi yomo no kuninaka to
Ō Yamato Hidaka Mi no Kuni o
Yasukuni to sadame matsurite

To govern the land below the Heavens,
A majestic shrine was erected by the people.
The main pillar of the shrine is rooted into the rock of the Earth
and rises splendidly to the Heavens.
The roof's majestic crossbeams extending as far as the Expanse
of High Heaven.
Sumemima no Mikoto dwells in this sacred hall to serve and rule
the Land.
Shitatsu iwane ni miyabashira futoshiki tate
Takama no Hara ni chigi takashirite
Sumemima no Mikoto no mizu no miaraka tsukae matsurite

The land shall prosper under the divine protection of the
Heavenly Kami and the blessing of the kami of the sun.
Following the ways of Nature, the realm shall know peace and
stability.
Ame no mikage hi no mikage to kakuri mashite
Yasukuni to taira keku shiroshi mesan kunuchi ni
Nari iden ame no masuhito ra ga

天(あま)つ罪(つみ)と畔(あ)放(はな)ち溝(みぞ)埋(う)め樋(ひ)放(はな)ち　頻(しき)蒔(ま)き串(くし)刺(ざ)し　生(いき)剥(は)ぎ逆(さか)

刺(は)ぎ　屎(くそ)戸(へ)許(こ)々(こ)太(だ)久(く)の罪(つみ)を　天(あま)つ罪(つみ)と宣(の)り別(わ)けて　國(くに)つ

罪(つみ)とは　生(いき)膚(はだ)断(た)ち　死(しに)膚(はだ)断(た)ち　白(しら)人(びと)胡(こ)久(く)美(み)　己(おの)が母(はは)犯(おか)せ

る罪(つみ)　己(おの)が子(こ)犯(おか)せる罪(つみ)　母(はは)と子(こ)と犯(おか)せる罪(つみ)　子(こ)と母(はは)と犯(おか)せ

る罪(つみ)　畜(けもの)犯(おか)せる罪(つみ)　昆(は)虫(ふむし)の災(わざはひ)　高(たか)つ神(かみ)の災(わざはひ)　高(たか)つ鳥(とり)の

12

Knowingly or unknowingly, however, people may from time to
  time commit transgressions and offenses;
Heavenly offenses such as those committed in the Expanse of
  High Heaven where
The fields were destroyed,
The animals debased, and
The Heavenly palace defiled.
Ayamachi okashiken kusagusa no tsumi goto wa
Amatsu tsumi to ahanachi mizoume hihanachi
Shikimaki kushizashi ikihagi sakahagi
Kusohe kokodaku no tsumi o
Amatsu tsumi to nori wakete

Sins of great extremes may occur—sins against Heaven
And sins against Earth,
Where blood flows from the living and from the dead;
And mothers and children,
Our source and our future—
Even the beasts of the land—
May be treated with disregard.
Kunitsu tsumi to wa
Ikihada tachi shinihada tachi
Shirahito kokumi
Onoga haha okaseru tsumi
Onoga ko okaseru tsumi
Haha to ko to okaseru tsumi
Ko to haha to okaseru tsumi
Kemono okaseru tsumi

災　畜仆し蠱物せる罪　許々太久の罪出でむ此く出でば

天つ宮事以ちて　天つ金木を本打ち切り　末打ち斷ちて

千座の置座に置き足らはして　天つ菅麻を本刈り斷ち　末

刈り切りて八針に取り辟きて　天つ祝詞の太祝詞事を宣れ

14

Great adversity may transpire on the Earth—
Calamities from insects and things of the air.
Misfortune and great sorrow may fall upon all beings,
For disregard of the order of Nature brings sorrow and darkness.
Hau mushi no wazawai
Takatsu kami no wazawai
Takatsu tori no wazawai
Kemono taoshi majimono seru tsumi
Kokodaku no tsumi iden kaku ideba

Whensoever such darkness needs to be swept away,
The Kannushi for the people of the Ancient Land shall make
    offerings—
The tops and the bottoms shall be clipped from golden trees and
    placed on an array of a thousand offering tables.
And the Heavenly Norito, the sacred liturgy, shall be recited
    solemnly in a great, majestic ritual,
Beseeching the kami to restore the order of Nature.
Amatsu miyagoto mochite
Amatsu kanagi o moto uchi kiri sue uchi tachite
Chikura no okikura ni oki tarawashite
Amatsu sugaso o moto kari tachi
Sue kari kirite yahari ni tori sakite
Amatsu norito no futo norito goto o nore.

[pause]

此く宣らば　天つ神は天の磐門を押し披きて　天の八重雲を伊頭の千別きに千別きて　聞こし食さむ　國つ神は高山の末　短山の末に上り坐して　高山の伊褒理　短山の伊褒理を　掻き分けて　聞こし食さむ　此く聞こし食してば

When these sacred words are pronounced,
The kami of Heaven will push open the Heavenly gates;
Kaku noraba amatsu kami wa ame no iwato o oshi hirakite *
Ame no yaegumo o Izu no chiwaki ni chiwakite
Kikoshi mesan

Heaven's eight-fold clouds will part,
And the kami shall lend ear to the sacred words.
The kami of the Earth shall climb to the tops of the high
    mountains and to the tops of the low mountains,
Dividing and sweeping away the mists of the high mountains and
    the mists of the low mountains,
Restoring clarity.
Kunitsu kami wa takayama no sue
Hikiyama no sue ni nobori mashite
Takayama no ibori
Hikiyama no ibori o
Kaki wakete
Kikoshi mesan

* When recited in a group, this phrase is read only by Saishu

罪と言ふ罪は在らじと　科戸の風の天の八重雲を　吹き放つ

事の如く　朝の御霧夕の御霧を　朝風夕風の吹き拂ふ事の

如く　大津邊に居る大船を　舳解き放ち艫解き放ちて　大

海原に押し放つ事の如く　彼方の繁木が本を　燒鎌の敏鎌

以ちて打ち掃ふ事の如く　遺る罪は在らじと　祓へ給ひ清

The kami shall lend ear to the sacred words.
No offences shall remain unpurged.
They shall be scattered and blown afar by Heaven's winds
   descending through the eight-fold clouds.
Kaku kikoshi meshiteba
Tsumi to yū tsumi wa arajito
Shinado no kaze no ame no yaegumo o
Fuki hanatsu koto no gotoku

Morning mists shall be cleared by the morning winds,
Just as the mists of evening shall be swept away by evening
   winds.
Ashita no migiri yūbe no migiri o
Asakaze yūkaze no fukiharō koto no gotoku

As a large ship anchored in a harbour casts off the moorings from
   its bow and is released into the great expanse of ocean,
So shall we be released of our impurities.
Ōtsube ni oru ōfune o
Hetoki hanachi tomo toki hanachite
Ō unabara ni oshi hanatsu koto no gotoku

As the trees of the thick grove rooted yonder are cleared away
   with a sharp sickle—
So shall our offences be purged and swept away.
Ochikata no shigeki ga moto o
Yakigama no togama mochite
Uchi harō koto no gotoku

We pray that these impurities be swept away and that
The kami grant us purification to restore the natural order.
Nokoru tsumi wa arajito
Harae tamai kiyome tamō koto o

め給ふ事を　高山の末短山の末より　佐久那太理に落ち多

岐つ　速川の瀬に坐す　瀬織津比賣と言ふ神　大海原に持

ち出でなむ　此く持ち出で往なば　荒潮の潮の八百道の八潮

道の潮の八百會に坐す　速開都比賣と言ふ神　持ち加加呑み

てむ　此く加加呑みてば　氣吹戸に坐す氣吹戸主と言ふ神

20

Let the impurities be swept away by the kami Seoritsu Hime
Who dwells in the swift rivers that cascade from the top of the
   high mountains and from the top of the low mountains,
Carrying the impurities out to the great expanse of ocean;
Takayama no sue hikiyama no sue yori
Saku nadari ni ochi tagitsu
Hayakawa no se ni masu
Seoritsu Hime to yū kami
Ō unabara ni mochi ide nan
Kaku mochi ide inaba

There, where the river meets the great sea,
Hayakitsu Hime, who dwells within the whirling myriad of tides,
Shall open wide and swallow the impurities;
Ara shio no shio no yaoji no
Ya shioji no shio no
Yao ai ni masu
Haya Akitsu Hime to yū kami
Mochi kaka nomi ten

Let the door open, then, from the bottom country,
And the kami called Ibukido Nushi shall cause great winds to
   expel the impurities to the root country.
Kaku kaka nomi teba
Ibukido ni masu Ibukido Nushi to yū kami
Ne no kuni soko no kuni ni ibuki hanachiten

根國底國（ねのくにそこのくに）に氣吹（いぶ）き放（はな）ちてむ　此（か）く氣吹（いぶ）き放（はな）ちてば　根國底國（ねのくにそこのくに）

に坐（ま）す　速佐須良比賣（はやさすらひめ）と言（い）ふ神（かみ）　持（も）ち佐須良（さすら）ひ失（うしな）ひてむ　此（か）

く佐須良（さすら）ひ失（うしな）ひてば　罪（つみ）と言（い）ふ罪（つみ）は在（あ）らじと　祓（はら）へ給（たま）ひ清（きよ）め

給（たま）ふ事（こと）を　天津神（あまつかみ）　國津神（くにつかみ）　八百万（やほよろず）の神等（かみたち）共（とも）に　聞（き）こし食（め）

せと白（まを）す

There, the kami called Haya Sasura Hime, the quiet wanderer of
the root country, will sieze and dissolve the impurities,
Ridding us of imperfection and returning us to our pristine
natural state.
Kaku ibuki hanachiteba
Ne no kuni soko no kuni ni masu
Haya Sasura Hime to yū kami
Mochi sasurai ushinai ten
Kaku sasurai ushinai teba
Tsumi to yū tsumi wa arajito

Grant us purification, grant us clarity.
We pray to the Heavenly Kami and to the Earthly Kami—
To all the myriad of kami we recite this norito with awe and
reverence.
Please hear these humble words.
Harae tamai kiyome tamō koto o
Amatsu kami
Kunitsu kami
Yaoyorozu no kamitachi tomo ni
Kikoshi mese to maosu.

敬神生活の綱領

一、神の恵みと祖先の恩とに感謝し、
明き清きまことを以て祭祀にいそしむこと。

一、世のため人のために奉仕し、
神のみこともちとして世をつくり固め成すこと。

一、大御心をいただきてむつび和らぎ、
国の隆昌と世界の共存共栄とを祈ること。

DECLARATION OF FAITH

Commitment of Life Devotion
KEI SHIN SEIKATSU NO KŌRYŌ

I am grateful for the blessings of the kami and my ancestors
And will practice my faith with brightness, purity, and sincerity.
Kami no megumi to sosen no on to ni kanshashi
Akaki kiyoki makoto o motte saishi ni isoshimu koto.

I will dedicate myself to serve and benefit the world and all
   peoples.
I will fulfill my life mission as guided by the kami, dedicating
   myself with sincerity to achieve peace for the world and for my
   nation.
Yo no tame hito no tame ni hōshishi
Kami no mikoto mochi toshite yo o tsukuri katame nasu koto.

From my heart, I will humbly follow and respect the kami,
Praying for harmony, prosperity, and peace for all nations of the
   world.
Ō mikokoro o itadakite mutsubi yawaragi
Kuni no ryūshō to sekai no kyōson kyōei to o inoru koto.

(pause, and continue to next section)

敬神生活の信条

一、猿田彦大神と天之鈿女命の御神霊を崇め敬い

天つ神地つ神八百萬神に感謝と祈りを捧げること。

一、猿田彦大神と天之鈿女命の御神徳を畏み奉り

神の子としての使命を努め果すこと。

一、猿田彦大神と天之鈿女命の御神導を戴き持ち

万有神化を念願として働き尽くすこと。

26

Articles of Faith
KEI SHIN SEIKATSU NO SHINJŌ

I revere the divine spirits of Sarutahiko no Ō Kami and Ame no
   Uzume no Mikoto;
I dedicate my prayers and gratitude to the Heavenly Kami, the
   Earthly Kami, and to the myriad of kami.
**Sarutahiko no Ō Kami to Ame no Uzume no Mikoto no
   mitama o agame uyamai**
**Amatsu kami kunitsu kami yaoyorozu no kami ni kansha to
   inori o sasageru koto.**

I will follow the sacred teachings of Sarutahiko no Ō Kami and
   Ame no Uzume no Mikoto;
I will strive to accomplish my purpose as a child and descendant
   of the kami.
**Sarutahiko no Ō Kami to Ame no Uzume no Mikoto no
   miitsu o kashikomi matsuri**
Kami no ko to shite no shimei o tsutome hatasu koto.

I accept and follow the guidance of Sarutahiko no Ō Kami and
   Ame no Uzume no Mikoto;
I will strive, through purification, to activate the kami within all
   beings and throughout Nature, thereby restoring divinity to all
   things.
**Sarutahiko no Ō Kami to Ame no Uzume no Mikoto no
   michibiki o itadaki mochi**
Banyū shinka o nengan to shite hataraki tsukusu koto.

五種の神歌

宮川や清き流れの禊にて　祈らむ事の叶はぬはなし

橘の伊勢の椿の禊にて　今も清むる我が身なりけり

罪咎や　御幣の川に祓ふらむ　瀬織津姫の神のみいつに

かけ流す大本宮の鈴鹿川　千代萬世に罪は残さず

振り鳴らす　鈴の響に魂滿ちて　みたまのふゆを弥聞し食せ

28

Five Sacred Shinto Poems
GOSHU NO SHINKA

The sacred waters of misogi flow pure,
Bringing fulfillment to sincere prayer.
Miyagawa ya kiyoki nagare no misogi nite
Inoran koto no kanawanu wa nashi

Now my body, heart, and spirit will again be made pure
Through misogi of Tsubaki, ancient land of Ise, Tachibana.
Tachibana no Ise no Tsubaki no misogi nite
Ima mo kiyomuru waga mi narikeri

In the river impurities are swept from me as if purified by gohei
Amidst the shining light of Seoritsu Hime no Kami.
Tsumi toga ya onbe no kawa ni harōran
Seoritsu Hime no Kami no miitsu ni

The shining light flows from this kami's original palace, the
    River Suzuka.
The tsumi, the impurities, will be removed for a thousand—even
    a myriad—of generations.
Kakenagasu ōmoto miya no Suzuka Gawa
Chiyo yorozuyo ni tsumi wa nokosazu

My spirit overflows with resounding and shaking of suzu bells
    ringing;
The beautiful sound and vibration invigorate my soul.
In awe I speak; hear these reverent words.
Furi narasu suzu no hibiki ni tama michite
Mitama no fuyu o iya kikoshimese

十種祓詞（とくさのはらへのことば）

高天原（たかまのはら）に神留り坐す（かむづまます）　皇神等（すめかみたち）鋳顕給ふ（あらはしたま）　十種瑞津寶を以（とくさのみづのたから）も

ちて　天照國照彦天火明櫛玉饒速日尊（あまてるくにてるひこあめのほあかりくしたまにぎはやひのみこと）に　授給事誨て曰（さづけたまふことおしへ）（のたまはく）

汝此瑞津寶を以ちて（いましこのみづのたから）（も）　中津國に天降り蒼生を鎮納よ（なかつくに）（あまくだ）（あをひとぐさ）（しづめをさめ）

30

Words of Purification from Ten Sources
TOKUSA NO HARAE NO KOTOBA

In the Expanse of High Heaven dwell the exalted kami.
Takama no Hara ni kamu zumari masu

The august ancestral kami bestowed Tokusa Kandakara, the ten
treasures of renewal,
To Nigihayahi no Mikoto, the magnificent kami who shines with
the radiance of the Earth and of the Heavens,
Instructing him to descend to the center of the Ancient Land,
And to impart to the people of the Land this gift of renewal and
overflowing treasure,
To transmit the ancient teaching to calm the spirit and restore
vitality to the soul.
Sume kamitachi iarawashi tamō
Tokusa no mizu no takara o mochite
Amateru Kuniteru Hiko Ame no Ho Akari Kushitama
Nigihayahi no Mikoto ni
Sazuke tamō koto oshiete notamawaku
Imashi kono mizu no takara o mochite
Nakatsukuni ni ama kudari aohitogusa o shizume osameyo

蒼生及萬物の疫病辭阿羅婆　神寳を以ちて御倉板に鎮置き

て　魂魄鎮祭を爲て瑞津寳を布留部　其の神祝の詞に日

甲乙丙丁戊己庚辛壬癸　一二三四五六七八九十

瓊音布留部由良由良　如此祈所為婆死共更に蘇生なむと誨

32

Even if a myriad of illnesses occur,
The Kandakara, the kami treasure, will be a well-spring of calm,
  putting behind any illness or unease.
Make still and hold fast my spirit;
I vibrate my center with the treasure of renewal as
I chant the mystical words given by the kami—
Aohitogusa oyobi yorozu no mono no yamai no koto araba
Kamutakara o mochite mikuraita ni shizume okite
Mitama shizume no matsuri o
Nashite mizu no takara o furube
Sono kamuhogi no kotoba ni iwaku

Kinoe kinoto hinoe hinoto tsuchinoe tsuchinoto kanoe kanoto
  mizunoe mizunoto
HI FU MI YO I MU NA YA KO TO
Kinoe kinoto hinoe hinoto tsuchinoe tsuchinoto kanoe kanoto
  mizunoe mizunoto
HI FU MI YO I MU NA YA KO TO

The roots of this chant lay in shaking of the soul—enlivening of
  the spirit—and in the jewel of sacred, mystical sound.
The Kandakara will bring about renewal of life, even from
  death—
So it is taught.
Ni no oto furube yura yura
Kaku inori se ba makaru tomo sara ni ikinan to oshie tamō

給ふ　天神御祖御詔を禀給て　天磐船に乗りて　河内國河上

の哮峯に天降坐して　大和國排尾の山の麓　白庭の高庭に

遷坐して鎮齋奉り給ふ　號て石神大神と申奉り　代々神寶

を以ちて萬物の爲に布留部の神辭を以ちて　司と爲給ふ故

Nigihayahi no Mikoto humbly took the sacred teachings of the
ancestral kami and,
Descending as a passenger in a boat from the origin of Heaven,
Alighted at Ikarugamine at the upper reaches of the river in the
ancient land of Kawachi.

Ame no kami no mioya mikotonori o kake tamaite
Ame no iwa fune ni norite
Kawachi no kuni no kawa kami no
Ikarugamine ni ama kudari mashi mashite

There, in a high garden, radiant in illumination, at the foot of a
mountain on the Ancient Land's edge,
Nigihayahi no Mikoto was revered as the kami of Iso no Kami
Shrine.

Yamato no kuni hiki no yama no fumoto
Shironiwa no takaniwa ni
Utsushi mashimashite itsuki matsuri tamō
Nazukete Iso no Kami no Ō kami to moshi tatematsuri

Because of the Kandakara, the sacred kami treasure transmitted
to countless generations,
Because of this sacred chant and shaking of the soul which shall
quell even 10,000 things,
We revere this august kami in highest esteem as Furu no Mitama.

Yoyo kamutakara o mochite yorozu no mono no tame ni
furube no kamugoto o mochite
Tsukasa to nashi tamō yue ni Furu no Mitama no Kami to
uyamai tatematsuri

に布留御魂神と尊敬奉り　皇子大連大臣其神武を以ちて齋

に仕へ奉り給ふ　物部の神社天下　萬物聚類化出大元の

神寶は　所謂瀛都鏡　邊都鏡　八握劍　生玉　足玉

死反玉　道反玉　蛇比禮　蜂比禮　品品物比禮　更に

十種神　甲乙丙丁戊己庚辛壬癸　一二三四五六七八

36

The spiritually fierce kami and this sacred shrine have
  transmitted this practice to generations of sincere followers.
The Kandakara, the treasure of the kami, holds divine power to
  renew and transform even 10,000 things.
**Sume mikoto ōmuraji otodo sono kami takeki o mochite
  itsuki ni tsukae matsuri tamō**
Mononobe no kami no yashiro ame ga shita
**Yorozu no mono no tagui nari iden ō moto no kamutakara
  wa iwayuru**

Distant mirror; close, nearby mirror; sword to cut through
  negativity;
The jewel of growth and life; jewel of fulfillment; jewel to return
  from death; jewel to remain on the true path;
The gift to correct Earthly disaster; gift to correct disaster from
  the air;
Countless gifts of purification and protection.
Okitsu kagami hetsu kagami yatsuka no tsurugi
Iku tama taru tama makaru gaeshi no tama
Chi gaeshi no tama
Orochi no hire hachi no hire
Kusagusa no mono no hire

Ten sources of renewal from the kami:
Sara ni tokusa no kami

Kinoe kinoto hinoe hinoto tsuchinoe tsuchinoto kanoe kanoto
  mizunoe mizunoto
HI FU MI YO I MU NA YA KO TO
**Kinoe kinoto hinoe hinoto tsuchinoe tsuchinoto kanoe kanoto
  mizunoe mizunoto**
HI FU MI YO I MU NA YA KO TO

九十　瓊音布留部由良　と由良加之奉る事の由縁を以ちて

平けく所聞食と　命壽遠子孫繁栄常磐堅磐に　護給ひ　幸

へ給ひ　加持奉　神通神妙神力楫

In gratitude for this gift, I humbly offer the beautiful jewel of
   sacred sound, emanating from the gift of envigorating my
   spirit.
I humbly beseech you to grant longevity and prosperity to me
   and to my many descendants.
Grant me protection, grant me happiness.
I humbly offer my reverence and appreciation.
Ni no oto furube yura to yura
Kashi tatematsuru koto no yoshi o mochite
Taira keku kikoshimese to
Inochi nagaku shison hanei tokiwa kakiwa ni
Mamori tamai sakiwae tamai kaji tatematsuru

This mystery, which I share in common with the kami, is my
   rudder of strength.
Jin tsū jin myō shin riki kaji

ひふみ 祓 詞 （適度反復）
のはらへことば

ひふみよいむなやこともちろらねしきるゆゐつわぬそを

たはくめかうおゑにさりへてのますあせえほれけ

40

Hi Fu Mi Words of Purification
HI FU MI NO HARAE KOTOBA

(Sacred syllables to be chanted while tuning the vibration of
your voice to the divine)

Hi fu mi yo i mu na ya ko to
Mo chi ro ra ne shi ki
Ru yu i tsu wa nu so
O ta ha ku me ka u o e ni
Sa ri he te no ma su a se e ho re ke

三種 大祓（みくさの おほ はらひ）

（適度反復）

吐普加身（とほかみ）　依身多女（えみため）　坎艮震（かんこんしん）　巽離坤兌乾（そんりこんだけん）

祓ひ給へ（はらたま）　清めで給ふ（きよたま）

42

Three Sources of Purification
MIKUSA NO Ō HARAHI

Live in harmony with the way of Great Nature,
Moving with its changes
Tō kami
Emi tame

North, northeast, east, southeast
South, southwest, west, northwest—
From all corners of the universe,
Kan gon shin
Son rikon da ken

Take away all impurities of my self,
My home, and the world.
Harahi tamae
Kiyome de tamō

十種神寶大御名（適度反復）
とくさのかむだからのおほみな

瀛津鏡（おきつかがみ）
邊津鏡（へつかがみ）
八握劍（やつかのつるぎ）
生玉（いくたま）
足玉（たるたま）
死反玉（まかるがへしのたま）
道反玉（ちがへしのたま）

蛇比禮（おろちのひれ）
蜂比禮（はちのひれ）
品品物比禮（くさぐさのもののひれ）
布留部由良由良止布留部（ふるべゆらゆらとふるべ）

44

Ten Great Treasures from the Kami
TOKUSA NO KANDAKARA
NO Ō MINA

Distant mirror
Close, nearby mirror
Okitsu kagami
Hetsu kagami

Sword to cut through negativity
Yatsuka no tsurugi

Jewel of growth and life
Jewel of fulfillment
Iku tama
Taru tama

Jewel to return from death
Jewel to remain on the the true path
Makaru gaeshi no tama
Chi gaeshi no tama

Gift to correct Earthly disaster
Gift to correct disaster from the air
Orochi no hire
Hachi no hire

Countless gifts of purification and protection
Kusagusa no mono no hire

Give energy to my spirit with these gifts
Furube yura yura to furube

神拝詞（齊唱）

掛（か）けまくも畏（かしこ）き　椿大神社（つばきおほかみやしろ）の大前（おほまへ）を拝（をろが）み奉（まつ）りて　恐（かしこ）み恐（かしこ）み

も白（まを）さく　大神等（おほかみたち）の廣（ひろ）き厚（あつ）き御惠（みめぐみ）を　辱（かたじけな）み奉（まつ）り　高（たか）き尊（たふと）き神（み）

教（をしへ）のまにまに　天皇（すめらみこと）を仰（あほ）ぎ奉（まつ）り直（なほ）き正（ただ）しき真心（まごころ）もちて　誠（まこと）

46

Sacred Prayer
SHIN PAISHI

Humbly, I approach the kami in prayer.
I pray to the kami of Tsubaki Grand Shrine; speaking with
reverent heart, I present offerings and prayers.
I come in humility and with great respect.

Kakema kumo kashikoki
Tsubaki Ō Kami Yashiro no ōmae o orogami matsurite
Kashikomi kashikomi mo maosaku

I beseech all the kami to accept these offerings that are brought
with
Gratitude for the blessings and the noble teachings
That have been bestowed upon me.

**Ō kamitachi no hiroki atsuki mi megumi o katajikenami
matsuri**
Takaki tōtoki mioshie no mani mani

To the divine, exalted kami, I humbly offer my prayers.
Teach me to live with a pure and sincere heart.
Grant me perseverance and that my heart be genuine, childlike,
and true.
Grant that I stay on the path of sincerity and truth.
Grant that I be strong and diligent at my deeds.

**Sumera mikoto o aogi matsuri naoki tadashiki magokoro
mochite**
Makoto no michi ni tagō koto naku
Oimotsu waza ni hage mashime tamai

も白（ま）す

く身健（みすこやか）に　世のため人（ひと）のために盡（つく）さしめ給（たま）へと　恐（かしこ）み恐（かしこ）み

の道（みち）に違（たが）ふことなく　負（お）ひ持（も）つ業（わざ）に励（はげ）ましめ給（たま）ひ　家門高（いえかどたか）

48

Grant good health to my family; give them strength in spirit,
   mind, and body.
Grant that I may benefit and serve all mankind.
With awe and reverence, I humbly speak these words.
Ie kado takaku mi sukoyaka ni
Yo no tame hito no tame ni tsukusashime tamae to
Kashikomi kashikomi mo maosu

稱　言（齊唱）

布都御魂大神　布留御魂大神　布都斯御魂大神

輿玉猿田彦大神　宮比天鈿女命

大御名は稱へ奉りて　石上　椿大神等

大神大神稜威嚇灼尊哉

大神大神稜威嚇灼尊哉

大神大神稜威嚇灼尊哉

Words of Praise
TATAE GOTO

(Chant in Unison)

To all the kami of Iso no Kami Shrine
And of Tsubaki Grand Shrine—
Alight your spirit.
Futsu no Mitama no Ō Kami
Furu no Mitama no Ō Kami
Futsushi no Mitama no Ō Kami
Okitama Sarutahiko no Ō Kami
Miyabi Ame no Uzume no Mikoto
Ō mina wa tatae matsurite
Iso no Kami
Tsubaki no Ō Kamitachi

Ō Kami Ō Kami, guide and illuminate the way!
Ō Kami Ō Kami, guide and illuminate the way!
Ō Kami Ō Kami, guide and illuminate the way!
Ō Kami Ō Kami miitsu kagayaku tōtoshiya
Ō Kami Ō Kami miitsu kagayaku tōtoshiya
Ō Kami Ō Kami miitsu kagayaku tōtoshiya

六根清浄の勤行

道祖の神　天照皇大神の御旨を　傳へて教へ導き宣はく　人は

即ち天の下の神の　物なり　天地を造り成し給ふ　大宇宙

の分身なり氏子なり　宜く静ることを掌るべし　心は即ち

神と靈との元の主たり　汝等の心身を傷ましむること勿れ

52

The Practice for Purification of the
Six Roots of Our Being
ROKKONSHŌJŌ NO KINGYŌ

The Kami of Earth, Sarutahiko no Ō Kami, following the
 instructions of Amaterasu Ō Mi Kami,
Guides us by conveying the sacred teachings of the ancient way.
Dōso no Kami
Amaterashimasu Sume Ō Mi Kami no mimune o
Tsutaete oshie michibiki notamawaku

All people are the embodiment of the kami, having received the
 gift of birth and growth.
Heaven and Earth were brought to life by the kami.
Followers of the kami may receive this sacred teaching which
 will enable them to make their spirits quiet, calm.
**Hito wa sunawachi ame no shita no kami no mitama mono
 nari**
Ametsuchi o tsukuri nashi tamō
Dai uchū no bunshin nari ujiko nari
Yoroshiku shizumaru koto o tsukasadoru beshi

The foundation of the soul and of the kami resides in our hearts.
Neither thy heart nor thy body must suffer.
Kokoro wa sunawachi kami to kami to no moto no aruji tari
Nanjira no shinshin o itamashimuru koto nakare

此の故に目にもろもろの不淨を見て　心にもろもろの不淨を見ず

耳にもろもろの不淨を聞きて　心にもろもろの不淨を聞かず

鼻にもろもろの不淨を嗅ぎて　心にもろもろの不淨を嗅がず

口にもろもろの不淨を言いて　心にもろもろの不淨を言はず

身にもろもろの不淨にふれて　心にもろもろの不淨にふれず

The eye may see all sorts of impure actions,
But let not these sights defile the heart.
Kono yue ni me ni moromoro no fujō o mite
Kokoro ni moromoro no fujō o mizu

The ear may hear all sorts of impure sounds,
But let not the heart be made impure.
Mimi ni moromoro no fujō o kikite
Kokoro ni moromoro no fujō o kikazu

The nose may smell all sorts of impure odors,
But let not the heart be touched by these impurities.
Hana ni moromoro no fujō o kagite
Kokoro ni moromoro no fujō o kagazu

Mouths may say all sorts of impurities,
But let not these sayings defile the heart.
Kuchi ni moromoro no fujō o yūte
Kokoro ni moromoro no fujō o yuwazu

Although the body may be assaulted by all sorts of impure
  energy,
Let not these impurities enter the heart.
Mi ni moromoro no fujō ni furete
Kokoro ni moromoro no fujō ni furezu

意にもろもろの不淨を思ふとも　中心にもろもろの不淨を思は

ず　この時に清く潔よき事あり　もろもろの法は影と像の如し

清く淨ければ假にも穢るること無し　説を取らば得べからず

皆花よりぞ木の實とはなる　我が身は即ち六根清淨なり　六根

清淨なるが故に　五臓の神君安寧なり　五臓の神君安寧なるが

56

The heart may behold all sorts of impure thoughts,
But let not these impurities reach the center core of the heart.
These moments will be cleansed for those of pure heart.
Kokoro ni moromoro no fujō o omō tomo
Naka gokoro ni moromoro no fujō o omowazu
Kono toki ni kiyoku isagiyoki koto ari

These teachings embody the spirituality of life.
Impurities will be temporary, for there is an array of teachings
    that will deflect the wrong and reflect purification of the root,
    the core of the heart.
Moromoro no nori wa kage to katachi no gotoshi
Kiyoku kiyo kereba kari ni mo kegaruru koto nashi

Life cannot be understood merely through words;
Just as blossoms are the fruit of the tree,
So the six roots emanate from our very being.
Koto o toraba ube karazu
Mina hana yorizo ko no mi to wa naru
Waga mi wa sunawachi rokkonshōjō nari

Truly, purification of our six roots
Brings vitality and peace to our five senses.
Rokkonshōjō naru ga yue ni
Go zō no shinkun anrei nari

Our five senses shall know vitality and peace;
Thence shall we know our common root with the kami of Heaven
    and Earth.
Go zō no shinkun anrei naru ga
Yue ni tenchi no kami to dō kon nari

故に天地の神と同根なり　天地の神と同根なるが故に萬物の

靈と同體なり　萬物の靈と同體なるが　故に爲すところ希て

成就せずと云ふことなし

無上靈寶　信受奉行　天壤無窮　命運隆昌　神ながら靈通

祓ひ給へ　清め給へ　守り給へ

幸へ給へ　照し給へ　導き給へ

58

As we realize our common root with the kami of Heaven and
  Earth,
Thence shall we be united with the spirit of a myriad of sources
  throughout Nature.
Tenchi no kami to dōkon naru ga
Yue ni banbutsu no rei to dōtai nari

As we are united with the spirit of a myriad of sources
  throughout Nature,
Thence there will be no aspiration beyond our grasp.
Banbutsu no rei to dōtai naru ga
Yue ni nasu tokoro negōte jōju sezu to yū koto nashi

With humble soul, trust in the way of the kami and fulfill life's
  purpose with sincerity.
Faith is as eternal as Heaven and Earth.
Restore us to our original brightness, and
Grant us strength that we may overcome life's difficulties and
  live in harmony with the divine way of Great Nature.
Mu jō rei hō
Shin ju bu gyō
Ten jō mu kyū
Mei un ryū shō
Kannagara reitsū

Sweep the impurities from my being and purify my spirit;
Grant me protection; grant me happiness;
Bring brightness to my soul and give me guidance.
Harahi tamae kiyome tamae
Mamori tamae sakiwae tamae
Terashi tamae michibiki tamae

稲荷祝詞

掛巻も恐き　稲荷大神の大前に　恐み恐みも白く　朝に夕

に勤み務る　家の産業を緩事無く　怠事無く　彌奬めに奬

め賜ひ　彌助に助賜ひて　家門高く令吹興賜ひ　堅磐に

常磐に命長く　子孫の八十連屬に至まで　茂し八桑枝の如

60

Prayer of Inari
INARI NORITO

Humbly, I approach the kami of Inari in prayer.
With awe and reverence,
I humbly speak these words.
Kakemakumo kashikoki
Inari Ō Kami no ō mae ni
Kashikomi kashikomi mo maosaku

Morning and night, I will diligently work at my tasks,
My family will not lessen its focus, nor will we neglect any thing
    undone.
Ashita ni yūbe ni isoshimi tsutomuru
Ie no nariwai o yurumu koto naku
Okotaru koto naku

I pray that the kami bestow on me encouragement and support to
    meet all challenges.
Iya susume ni susume tamai
Iya tasuke ni tasuke tamaite

Grant that the divine winds bring prosperity to my family.
Bestow long life that is strong and solid.
Iekado takaku fuki oko sashime tamai
Kakiha ni tokiha ni inochi nagaku

Grant that my descendants, for countless generations,
Know protection, health, and longevity.
Uminoko no yasotsuzuki ni itaru made
Ikashi yakuwae no gotoku tachi sakaeshime tamai

く令立榮賜ひ　家にも身にも　枉神の枉事不令有　過犯

す事の有むをば　神直日大直日に見直聞直坐て　夜の守

日の守に守　幸へ賜へと　恐み恐みも白す

Grant us safety from malevolent kami, and grant that my home
   and my body be protected from any malevolent deeds.
If I commit an error, if I stray from my intended path,
I pray that the kami help me correct my way
That once again I may hear clearly,
That once again I may sit with open mind.
Ie ni mo mi ni mo
Magakami no magakoto ara shime zu
Ayamachi okasu koto no aramu o ba
Kannaobi ōnaobi ni minaoshi kikinaoshi mashite

Protect me in the night.
Protect me and shelter me in the day.
Grant me happiness.
With awe and reverence, I humbly speak these words.
Yo no mamori
Hi no mamori ni mamori
Sakiwae tamae to
Kashikomi kashikomi mo maosu

天神地祇祈念祝詞

上は高天の原を照らし　下は葦原の中つ國を輝やかし給

ふ　神風の伊勢国一の宮　地祇大本宮と稱へ奉る　椿大神

社に　神代ながらも齋ひ祭る　主神導きの道の祖　椿大明

神猿田彦大神　相殿に齋い祭る皇孫瓊々杵尊　御皇妃栲幡

Special Prayer to Kami of Heaven and Earth
TENSHIN CHIGI KINEN NORITO

Sarutahiko no Ō Kami shines up to the High Expanse of Heaven,
Casting illumination across the great Earthly realm of Ashihara
no Nakatsu Kuni.
Kami wa Takama no Hara o terashi
Shimo wa Ashihara no Nakatsu Kuni o
Kagayakashi tamō

Divine winds envelop Tsubaki Grand Shrine, the first shrine of
Ise,
The main shrine of all Earthly Kami where generations have
come to present offerings.
Sarutahiko no Ō Kami has been revered throughout the ages as
the principal kami of guidance throughout the Earth.
Kamikaze no Ise no kuni ichi no miya
Chigi dai hongu to tatae matsuru
Tsubaki Ō Kami Yashiro ni
Kami yo nagara mo iwai matsuru
Shushin michibiki no michi no oya
Tsubaki Dai Myō Jin Sarutahiko no Ō Kami

We respect and revere the noble spirits of other kami enshrined
here,
Sumemima Ninigi no Mikoto
And his esteemed mother, Taku Hatachiji Hime no Mikoto
Aidono ni iwai matsuru
Sumemima Ninigi no Mikoto
On haha Takuhata Chiji Hime no Mikoto

千々姫尊　配祀天之鈿女命　木花咲耶姫命　行満大明神

天津神地津神八百萬千五百萬の神々の尊き御靈を　かく

崇め敬ひ　仕へ奉る　　氏子信人崇敬者の生活活動事

業　またその命運念願希望の上に　奇しくも妙なる神智靈

66

Also enshrined are
Ame no Uzume no Mikoto
Kono Hana Sakuya Hime no Mikoto, and
Gyōman Dai Myō Jin
Haishi niwa Ame no Uzume no Mikoto
Kono Hana Sakuya Hime no Mikoto
Gyōman Dai Myō Jin

Heavenly Kami, Earthly Kami
All the many myriad of kami
The mitama of many exalted kami:
We reverently offer our respect.
Amatsu kami kunitsu kami
Yaoyorozu
Chii ho yorozu no kamigami no tōtoki mitama o
Kaku agame uyamai

Grant to these sincere Shinto followers that our hearts' desires be
    realized
And that we be guided in wisdom and ability to receive spiritual
    fulfillment.
Tsukae matsuru **
Ujiko mamebito sū keisha no sei katsu katsudō jigyō
Mata sono meiun nengan kibō no ue ni
Kusushikumo taenaru shinchi reinō o kagafurase tamai

**for specific prayer request, insert the following text and the
    petitioner's name:

Mamebito tachi no mina o ōmae ni noriaguru
[insert petitioner's name]
korera imashi ōmae ni maimōde taru

能を蒙らせ給ひ　神ながら諸々の障害を祓ひ除き　諸行

健やかに改め匡し　天地と同根一體の靈驗を體得せしめ給

ひ　天つ日の大神　天照らし坐す皇大神の身旨のまにまに

本を本と成し　末を末と成し　左を左と成し　右を右と成

し　何事をも見直し聞き直し給ひて　日毎夜毎魔性のものに

68

We beseech the kami to purify our path so that we may fulfill our
   divine mission.
Remove every sort of obstacle,
Correct our path for renewed health.
We originate from the same root as Heaven and Earth;
We pray that the kami help us to realize spiritual fullness.
Kannagara moromoro no sawari o harai nozoki
Shogyō sukoyaka ni aratame tadashi
Ametsuchi to dōkon ittai no
Reiken o taitoku seshime tamai

Amaterasu Ō Kami, shining from the Heavens,
Imparted teachings that we should restore all things to their
   original state:
Restore the beginning as the beginning;
Restore the end as the end;
Restore the left as the left;
Restore the right as the right.
Whatever needs to be restored,
Grant that we may hear and understand the correct way.
Amatsu Hi no Ō Kami
Amaterashi Masu Sumera Ō Mi Kami no
Mimune no manimani
Moto o moto to nashi
Sue o sue to nashi
Hidari o hidari to nashi
Migiri o migiri to nashi
Nanigoto o mo minaoshi kikinaoshi tamaite

犯（おか）さるる事（こと）なく　強（つよ）く正（ただ）しく向榮（むくさか）に　守（まも）り幸（さきわ）へ導（みちび）き給（たま）ひ　天（てん）

則（そく）に基（もと）づきて　地行（ちぎょう）の隆昌（りゅうしょう）につとめ　克（よ）くその任務役割（にんむやくわり）を

果（は）たし以（もっ）て　天禄永昌（てんろくえいしょう）　福徳円滿（ふくとくえんまん）　無病息災（むびょうそくさい）　衣食充實（いしょくじゅうじつ）

住宅平安（じゅうたくへいあん）　家内安全（かないあんぜん）　交通安全（こうつうあんぜん）　家業繁栄（かぎょうはんえい）に　あらしめ給（たま）ひ

70

Every day, every night,
Let us not be affected by evil things.
Turn us toward prosperity with strength and righteousness.
Grant us protection, happiness, and guidance.
Higoto yogoto
Mashō no mono ni okasaruru koto naku
Tsuyoku tadashiku mukusaka ni
Mamori sakiwae michibiki tamai

Lead us to carry out our life mission with strength and clarity.
Help us to follow the teachings of Heaven,
To strive for peace and to carry out our missions and
   responsibilities with humility.
Tensoku ni motozukite
Chigyō no ryūshō ni tsutome
Yoku sono ninmu yakuwari o hatashi motte

Longevity of Heaven's brightness
Fullness of happiness and virtue
Freedom from illness and disaster
Fullfillment of our basic needs
Peace and tranquility in our homes
Safety for our families
Safety in our travels
Prosperity in our business;
Grant all these blessings.
Tenroku eisho
Fukutoku enman
Mubyō sokusai
Ishoku jūjitsu
Jūtaku heian
Kanai anzen
Kōtsū anzen
Kagyō hanei ni
Arashime tamai

71

七難即滅して　七福即生せしめ　悪因を断絶して　善根を

彌榮にあらしめ給ひ　神州を修理して民族協和　萬代泰

平の基を　この國土に築き　國家隆昌　世界一家　天地平

安　一切悉々く皆　神の氏子として　神ながらの悦びに

生き往くことを得せしめ給ひ　各も各もその念願成就の

As you banish seven problems,
Give birth to seven blessings.
Cut away and separate evil causes from us;
Make good roots flourish for eternity.
Shichi nan sokumetsu shite
Shichi fuku sokushō seshime
Akuin o danzetsu shite
Zenkon o iyasakae ni arashime tamai

Grant that the countries of this divine world govern with a hand
   of harmony and truth,
That countless generations may know peace and harmony
   throughout the land.
Shinshū o shuri shite minzoku kyōwa
Bandai taihei no motoi o
Kono kokudo ni kizuki

Build a world rooted in prosperity for all generations to come
Bestow peace throughout Heaven and Earth.
Kokka ryūshō
Sekai ikka
Tenchi heian

Enable us to rejoice in the kami and in all living things;
May we realize each and every desire of our hearts.
Issai kotogotoku mina
Kami no ujiko toshite
Kannagara no yorokobi ni
Iki yuku koto o e seshime tamai
Onomo onomo sono nengan jōju no tame

SHINTO NORITO

爲め　夜の守り　日の守りに守り　導き幸へ給へと祈り申

す事を　導きの神の御導きのまにまに　八百萬の神等共に

聞し食し相諾ひ知ろし食し給へと　畏み畏みも申す

無上靈寶　信受奉行　天壤無窮

命運隆昌　無難入神　化生安樂

74

Protect us in the night.
Protect and shelter us in the day.
Guide us and grant us happiness.
Humbly, we pray for these things.
Yo no mamori
Hi no mamori ni mamori
Michibiki sakiwae tamae to
Inori maosu koto o

Great kami of guidance,
Together with eight myriad of kami,
Bestow on us an array of guidance.
Michibiki no kami no
On michibiki no manimani
Yaoyorozu no kamitachi tomo ni

We beseech the kami to unite and hear our prayers.
Humbly, respectfully, we speak this prayer.
Kikoshimeshi ai uzunai shiroshi meshi tamae to
Kashikomi kashikomi mo maosu

With humble soul, trust in the way of the kami and fulfill life's
    purpose with sincerity.
Faith is as eternal as Heaven and Earth.
Restore us to our original brightness, and grant us strength that
    we may overcome life's difficulties and live in harmony with
    the divine spirit of Great Nature.
Mu jō rei hō
Shin ju bu gyō
Ten jō mu kyū
Mei un ryū shō
Bu nan nyū shin
Ka shō an raku

道祖　猿田彦大明神　道祖　猿田彦大明神

道祖　猿田彦大明神

祓へ給へ清め給へ　六根清浄　祓へ給へ清め給へ　六根清

淨　祓へ給へ清め給へ　六根清浄

妙法示現神変神通力　妙法示現神変神通力

妙法示現神変神通力

守り導き給へ

Sarutahiko, Great Bright Being.
Dōso Sarutahiko Dai Myō Jin
Dōso Sarutahiko Dai Myō Jin
Dōso Sarutahiko Dai Myō Jin

Sweep impurities from my being and purify the six roots of my
  spirit.
Harae tamae kiyome tamae rokkonshōjō
Harae tamae kiyome tamae rokkonshōjō
Harae tamae kiyome tamae rokkonshōjō

May we follow kannagara, the way of the universe, the kami
  manifesting divine power in our beings.
Myō hō ji gen jin pen jin tsū riki
Myō hō ji gen jin pen jin tsū riki
Myō hō ji gen jin pen jin tsū riki

Bestow protection and guidance on us all.
Mamori michibiki tamae

祓　詞
はらへの　ことば

掛けまくも畏き　伊邪那岐大神　筑紫の日向の　橘　小戸の阿

波岐原に　御禊祓ひ給ひし時に生り坐せる　祓戸の大神等

諸々の禍事罪穢有らむをば　祓へ給ひ清め給へと白す事を

聞こし食せと　恐み恐みも白す

78

Words of Purification
HARAE NO KOTOBA

Humbly, I approach the kami in prayer.
Kakemakumo kashikoki

Our great ancestral kami Izanagi no Ō Kami
Performed misogi at Ahagihara of Odo, Tachibana of Himuka, in
    Tsukushi of the Ancient Land
Where his very being was cleansed by many Great Kami of
    Purification.
Izanagi no Ō Kami
Tsukushi no Himuka no
Tachibana no Odo no Ahagihara ni
Misogi harahi tamaishi toki ni nari maseru
Haraedo no Ō Kamitachi

I humbly beseech the kami to cleanse me of all impurities
Within myself, in my relationships with others, and
Between myself and the way of Great Nature.
Moromoro no magagoto tsumi kegare aramu o ba
Harae tamai kiyome tamae to
Maosu koto o

Hear these modest words.
Humbly, reverently, I speak this prayer.
Kikoshi meseto
Kashikomi kashikomi mo maosu

天地一切清浄祓

天清浄地清浄内外清浄　六根清浄と祓給ふ　天清浄とは

天の七曜九曜二十八宿を　清め　地清浄とは　地の神

三十六神を　清め　内外清浄とは　家内三寶大荒神を

清め　六根清浄とは　其身其體の穢を　祓給清め給ふ

Unification of Heaven and Earth's Purity
TENCHI ISSAI SHŌJŌ HARAI

Purity of Heaven, purity of Earth,
Within and without,
Sweep impurities entirely from all beings.
Tenshōjō chishōjō naigeshōjō
Rokkonshōjō to harai tamō

Bestow clarity on our era, our destiny, and our universe;
Remove obstacles and impurities from this Earth.
Tenshōjō to wa
Ten no shichiyō kuyō nijūhasshuku o
Kiyome

The kami of the Earth, the thirty-six primary guardians—
Chishōjō to wa
Chi no kami sanjūroku jin o
Kiyome

Sweep impurities from within and without our homes,
And purify the kami of Three Treasures.
Naigeshōjō to wa
Kanai sanbō dai kōjin o
Kiyome

Purify the six roots of our being;
Remove obstacles from our path;
Sweep away impurities and bestow clarity.
Rokkonshōjō to wa
Sono mi sono tai no kegare o
Harai tamae kiyome tamō

事の由を　八百萬の神等　諸共に小男鹿の八の御耳を

振立て　聞し食と申す

We pray to the myriad of kami to
Bring these things to pass.
Koto no yoshi o
Yaoyorozu no kamitachi

Every creature of this Earth fervently stands before you;
Humbly, reverently we speak these words.
Morotomo ni saoshika no yatsu no on mimi o furitate te
Kikoshimese to maosu

一切成就祓
いっ さい じょうじゅのはらひ

穢とはあらじ内外の玉垣
きたなき　うち と　たま がき

極て汚も滞無れば
きわめ　きたなき　たまり なけ

清淨と申す
きよくきよし　まを

84

Prayer for Complete Purification
ISSAI JŌJŪ NO HARAI

Even for things most impure,
Even if things are left undone and in disarray,
Respectfully I ask that the kami hear these words and grant
   complete purification and clarity,
Both within and without.

Kiwamete kitanaki mo tamari nakere ba
Kitanaki to wa araji uchi to no tamagaki
Kiyoku kiyoshi to maosu.

九字法（くじほう）

刀印（とういん）を以（もっ）って行（おこな）ふ

◎ 臨兵闘者階陳裂在前（りんびょうとうしゃかいじんれつざいぜん）

◎ 妙法示現神変神通力（みょうほうじげんじんぺんじんつうりき）

◎ 道祖猿田彦大明神（どうそさるたひこだいみょうじん）（三回唱える）

◎ 祓（はら）へ給（たま）ひ　清（きよ）め給（たま）へ　六根清浄（ろっこんしょうじょう）（三回唱える）

Nine Character Practice
(Chant for Protective Energy)
KUJI HŌ

(NOTE: Chant with spiritual vibration to invoke protection of
the kami)
(Tōin o motte okonau)

I shall stand with might before adversity, with courage and
confidence, moving forward with strength.
Rin pyo tō sha kai jin retsu zai zen
Rin pyo tō sha kai jin retsu zai zen
Rin pyo tō sha kai jin retsu zai zen

I shall follow kannagara, the way of the universe, the kami
manifesting divine power in my being.
Myō hō ji gen jin pen jin tsū riki
Myō hō ji gen jin pen jin tsū riki
Myō hō ji gen jin pen jin tsū riki

Sarutahiko, Great Bright Being,
Dōso Sarutahiko Dai Myō Jin
Dōso Sarutahiko Dai Myō Jin
Dōso Sarutahiko Dai Myō Jin

Sweep impurities from my being and purify the six roots of my
spirit.
Harae tamai kiyome tamae rokkonshōjō
Harae tamai kiyome tamae rokkonshōjō
Harae tamai kiyome tamae rokkonshōjō

87

略拝詞
（りゃくはいし）

道祖猿田彦大明神（どうそさるたひこだいみょうじん）

道祖猿田彦大明神（どうそさるたひこだいみょうじん）

道祖猿田彦大明神（どうそさるたひこだいみょうじん）

祓へ給ひ（はらへたまひ）　清め給へ（きよめたまへ）　守り給ひ（まもりたまひ）

幸へ給へ（さきはへたまへ）　照し給ひ（てらしたまひ）　導き給へ（みちびきたまへ）

88

Short Prayer
RYAKU HAISHI

Sarutahiko, Great Bright Being.
Sarutahiko, Great Bright Being.
Sarutahiko, Great Bright Being.
Dōso Sarutahiko Dai Myō Jin
Dōso Sarutahiko Dai Myō Jin
Dōso Sarutahiko Dai Myō Jin

Sweep the impurities from my being and purify my spirit;
Grant me protection; grant me happiness;
Restore brightness to my soul and give me guidance.
Harae tamai kiyome tamae mamori tamai
Sakiwae tamae terashi tamai michibiki tamae

日拝詞

上は高天原を照らし　下は葦原の中つ國を　輝やかし給ふ　神風の伊勢国一の宮　椿大明神猿田彦大神　配祀天之鈿女命の大前を　拝み奉りて　恐み恐みも白さく　大神等の廣き厚き　御惠を辱み奉り　高き尊き御教のまにまに

90

Daily Prayer
NIPPAISHI

Sarutahiko no Ō Kami shines up to the Expanse of High Heaven,
Casting illumination across the great Earthly realm of the
  Ancient Land.
Kami wa Takama no Hara o terashi
Shimo wa Ashihara no Nakatsu Kuni o
Kagayakashi tamō

Sacred winds envelop Tsubaki Grand Shrine, the first shrine of
  Ise,
Where dwells the great, bright deity Sarutahiko no Ō Kami and
  Ame no Uzume no Mikoto.
Before these kami I pray and present my offerings,
Speaking humbly and with a reverent heart.
Kamikaze no Ise no kuni ichi no miya
Tsubaki Dai Myo Jin Sarutahiko no Ō Kami
Haishi Ame no Uzume no Mikoto no ōmae o
Orogami matsurite
Kashikomi kashikomi mo maosaku

To all the divine kami throughout Heaven and Earth,
I gratefully offer my service and request that you bestow
  blessings on me.
Ō kamitachi no hiroki atsuki
Mi megumi o katajikenami matsuri

With great respect, I seek to follow the teachings of the kami in
  order that I may restore my spirit to the correct path of
Purity, brightness, righteousness, and straightforwardness.
Takaki tōtoki mioshie no manimani
Naoki tadashiki magokoro mochite

直き正しき眞心もちて　誠の道に違ふことなく　負ひ持

つ業に勵ましめ給ひ　家門高く身健に ﹕﹕人のために

盡さしめ給へと　恐み恐みも白す

Grant that I live with a true and just heart;
Keep me from harming others; and grant that I bear my
  responsibilities with diligence and sincerity.
Makoto no michi ni tagō kotonaku
Oi motsu waza ni hagemashime tamai

I pray that my home be blessed and that my family be granted
  good health.
I will work to serve others and to benefit my world and mankind;
Ie kado takaku mi sukoyaka ni
Yo no tame hito no tame ni tsuku sashime tamae to

Humbly, reverently, I speak these words.
Kashikomi kashikomi mo maosu

略日拝詞

上（かみ）は高天原（たかまのはら）を照（て）らし　下（しも）は葦原（あしはら）の中（なか）つ國（くに）を　輝（かが）やかし給（たも）ふ　神（かみ）

風（かぜ）の伊勢（いせ）国（くに）一（いち）の宮（みや）　椿大明神（つばきだいみょうじん）猿田彦（さるたひこ）大神（のおほかみ）　祓（はら）へ給（たま）へ　清（きよ）め給（たま）

へ　守（まも）り給（たま）へ　幸（さきわ）へ給（たま）へ　照（て）らし給（たま）へ　導（みちび）き給（たま）へ　すがすがし

く健（すこ）やかに日毎（ひごと）夜毎（よごと）を　あらしめ給（たま）へと　恐（かしこ）み恐（かしこ）みも白（まを）す

94

Short Daily Prayer
RYAKU NIPPAISHI

Sarutahiko no Ō Kami shines up to the Expanse of High Heaven,
Casting illumination across the great Earthly realm of the
  Ancient Land.
Kami wa Takama no Hara o terashi
Shimo wa Ashihara no Nakatsu Kuni o
Kagayakashi tamō

Divine winds envelop Tsubaki Grand Shrine, the first shrine of
  Ise,
Where dwells the great, bright deity Sarutahiko no Ō Kami.
Kamikaze no Ise no kuni ichi no miya
Tsubaki Dai Myō Jin Sarutahiko no Ō Kami

Sweep the impurities from my being and purify my spirit;
Grant me protection; grant me happiness;
Restore brightness to my soul and give me guidance.
Harae tamae kiyome tamae mamori tamae
Sakiwae tamae terashi tamae michibiki tamae

Each day and each night,
Grant me good health and spiritual renewal;
Humbly, reverently, I speak these words.
Sugasugashiku sukoyaka ni higoto yogoto o
Arashime tamae to
Kashikomi kashikomi mo maosu

無上靈寶　信受奉行

天壤無窮　命運隆昌

無難入神　化生安樂

幸へ給へ　照し給へ　導き給へ

祓へ給へ　清め給へ　守り給へ

With humble soul, I will trust in the kami and fulfill my life's
purpose with sincerity.
Faith is as eternal as Heaven and Earth.
Restore me to my original brightness and
Grant me strength that I may overcome life's difficulties and live
in harmony with the divine way of Great Nature.
Mu jō rei hō shin ju bu gyō
Ten jō mu kyū mei un ryū shō
Bu nan nyū shin ka shō an raku

Sweep the impurities from my being and purify my spirit;
Grant me protection; grant me happiness.
Bring brightness to my soul and give me guidance.
Harae tamae kiyome tamae mamori tamae
Sakiwae tamae terashi tamae michibiki tamae

神棚拝詞

此の神床に坐す　掛けまくも畏き　天つ神天照大御神　國つ神

猿田彦大神　産土大神　八百萬神等の大前を拝み奉りて　恐

み恐みも白さく　大神等の廣き厚き御惠を　辱み奉り　高き

98

Kamidana Prayer
KAMIDANA HAISHI

On this shelf dwell esteemed kami.
Humbly, I approach in prayer.
I pray to Amaterasu Ō Mi Kami, leader of all Heavenly deities;
To Sarutahiko no Ō Kami, leader of all Earthly deities;
Kore no kamudoko ni masu
Kakemakumo kashikoki
Amatsu kami Amaterasu Ō Mi Kami
Kunitsu kami Sarutahiko no Ō Kami

To my own Guardian Kami, and to the countless myriad of kami.
I speak to all the kami with a reverent heart, and to these kami
I humbly offer my prayers.
I come in humility and with great respect.
Ubusuna no Ō Kami
Yaoyorozu no kamitachi no ōmae o orogami matsurite
Kashikomi kashikomi mo maosaku

I beseech all the kami to accept these offerings that I present with
  heart-felt gratitude for the blessings that have been bestowed
  on me.
Ō kamitachi no hiroki atsuki mi megumi o
Katajikenami matsuri

尊き御教のまにまに　直き正しき眞心をもちて　誠の道に違ふ

ことなく　負ひ持つ業に勵ましめ給ひ　家門高く身健に　世の

ため　人のために　盡さしめ給へと　恐み恐みも白す

To all the divine kami, I pray that you bestow blessings;
I will be reverently grateful for your favors.
Grant me perseverance and that my heart by genuine, childlike,
   and true.
Grant that I stay on the path of sincerity and truth.
Takaki tōtoki mioshie no mani mani
Naoki tadashiki magokoro o mochite
Makoto no michi ni tagō kotonaku

Grant that I be strong and diligent at my deeds.
Grant good health to my family;
Give them strength in spirit, mind, and body.
Oimotsu waza ni hage mashime tamai
Ie kado takaku mi sukoyaka ni

Grant that I may benefit and serve all mankind.
Humbly, reverently, I speak these words.
Yo no tame hito no tame ni tsuku sashime tamae to
Kashikomi kashikomi mo maosu

祖霊拝詞（それいはいし）

代代（よよ）の先祖等（みおやたち）（何某の御霊（みたま））の御前（みまへ）を　拝み奉（まつ）りて慎（つつし）み敬（うやま）

ひも白（まを）さく　廣（ひろ）き厚（あつ）き御恵（みめぐみ）を　辱（かたじけな）み奉（まつ）り　高（たか）き尊（たふと）き家訓（みをしへ）のま

にまに　身（み）を慎（つつし）み業（わざ）に励（はげ）み　親族家族諸（うからやからもろ）諸心（もろこころ）を合（あは）せ　睦（むつ）び

102

Ancestral Prayer
SOREI HAISHI

I respectfully pray to the generations and generations of my
ancestors, and especially to the spirit of [insert name].
I present these offerings and prayers with humility and reverence.
Yoyo no mi oyatachi [nanigashi no mitama] no mimae o
Orogami matsurite tsutsushimi uyamai mo maosaku

I beseech you to accept these offerings that I present with heart-
felt gratitude for the multitude of blessings that have been
bestowed on me.
Hiroki atsuki mi megumi o katajikenami matsuri

Humbly, I ask that you impart to me your venerable teachings for
living with sincerity.
Takaki tōtoki mioshie no manimani

Encourage me in my efforts to live righteously,
To unite the hearts of my family members,
To live in harmony, with respect and service to others.
Mi o tsutsushimi waza ni hagemi
Ukara yakara moromoro kokoro o awase
Mutsubi nagomite
Uyamai tsukae matsuru sama o

和<ruby>な<rt>なご</rt></ruby>みて　敬<ruby>うやま<rt></rt></ruby>ひ仕<ruby>つか<rt></rt></ruby>へ奉<ruby>まつ<rt></rt></ruby>る状<ruby>さま<rt></rt></ruby>を　愛ぐしと見<ruby>み<rt></rt></ruby>そなはしまして

子孫<ruby>うみのこ<rt></rt></ruby>の八十續<ruby>やそつづぎ<rt></rt></ruby>に至<ruby>いた<rt></rt></ruby>るまで　家門<ruby>いへかど<rt></rt></ruby>高<ruby>たか<rt></rt></ruby>く立ち榮<ruby>さか<rt></rt></ruby>えしめ給<ruby>たま<rt></rt></ruby>へと

愼<ruby>つつし<rt></rt></ruby>み敬<ruby>うやま<rt></rt></ruby>ひも白<ruby>まを<rt></rt></ruby>す

Continue to protect and watch over my family and descendants;
Grant prosperity and respect to my family.
Megushi to miso nawashimashite
Umi noko no yasotsuzuki ni itaru made
Ie kado takaku tachi sakaeshime tamae to

I offer this prayer in humility and in reverence.
Tsutsushimi uyamai mo maosu

APPENDIX

APPENDIX A

PRONUNCIATION

Japanese words are actually fairly easy to pronounce, since our system of writing in English letters, or *romaji*, reflects the exact pronunciation. It is a very rhythmic language; the cadence is easy to follow.

If you learn the correct pronunciation of the vowel sounds and understand the *onsetsu* concept, you will find reading Japanese words in *romaji* quite simple.

Vowels

Vowel sounds remain unchanged, regardless of the combination with various consonants or other vowels.

a	pronounced like [a] in "father"
i	pronounced like [ee] in "meet"
u	pronounced like [oo] in "boot"
e	pronounced like [e] in "met"
o	pronounced like [o] in "over"

Onsetsu

Onsetsu is a basic unit of Japanese pronunciation, similar to a syllable. It represents one beat in the regular rhythm of Japanese, and therefore each *onsetsu* takes approximately the same amount of time to pronounce.

If two vowels are together, each vowel occupies one *onsetsu*; vowels are not blended as in the English language. Similarly, if two consonants are together, each one occupies one *onsetsu*.

Long vowels: In this text, when "o" is intended to be long, or to occupy 2 *onsetsu*, "ō" is used. Similarly, "ū" is pronounced with 2 *onsetsu* beats.

Examples are shown below, with each circle indicating one *onsetsu* unit:

•	• •	• •	• •	• • •
hi	ka mi	a me	yū	ta ka ra

• • •	• • •	• • • •	• • • • •
ri n go	ta t te	Ō Ka mi	o ka shi ke n

Thus, the following phrase, which is frequently used at the conclusion of a prayer, is pronounced as shown with the *onsetsu* symbols:

Kashikomi kashikomi mo maosu

• • • •	• • • •	•	• • •
ka shi ko mi	ka shi ko mi	mo	mao su

APPENDIX B

GLOSSARY

Amaterasu Ō Mi Kami The kami endowed with the virtue of the sun, whose name means "She Who Shines in the Heavens." She was so bright and radiant that her parents, Izanagi and Izanami, sent her up the Celestial ladder to Heaven where she rules the Heavenly Kami *(Amatsu Kami)*.

Amatsu Kami Heavenly Kami.

Ame no Uzume no Mikoto Kami of divine movement, entertainment, and marriage. When Amaterasu Ō Mi Kami hid herself in a cave, casting the world in darkness, Ame no Uzume no Mikoto performed a provoking and mirthful dance, enticing Amaterasu Ō Mi Kami to emerge from the cave out of curiosity. Wife of Sarutahiko no Ō Kami. Literal translation, Whirling From the Heavens.

Chinkon A meditation practice to calm and intensify the soul.

Chohai Morning ceremonial practice.

Gofu Paper inscribed with name of a kami that is placed over a doorway to a home, kitchen, or place of business to invoke protection by the kami.

Haishi Prayer; less formal than Norito.

Harahi, harai, harae Shinto purification, performed at the beginning of all ceremonies and for specific needs. In Shinto ceremony not only are the impurities, pollution, and misfortune of an individual removed, but impurities can also be removed from an entire community or nation for renewal of life energy and purity. Although all three terms are pronounced similarly, the written differentiation in Japanese is significant, hence in these translations the Romaji reflects the Japanese differentiation. *Harahi* refers to purification of an entire community or the world; *harahi* is purification of all things in nature as a result of unification of kami and mankind. *Harai* refers to purification of one's self. *Harae* refers to purification of a specific group, such as a family, parish, or community.

Haraigushi Used for purification, a wooden stick with *shide* (paper streamers) used to "sweep away" impurities. Sometimes *shide* are instead attached to an evergreen branch, which is then referred to as *ōnusa*.

Hatsuhoryo Donation to shrine when requesting special prayers or ceremony.

Izanagi no Mikoto and Izanami no Mikoto The first married couple in the Age of the Kami who were given the task of creating the world. They stood on the Floating Bridge of Heaven (*Ama no Ukihashi*) and stirred the oceans with a spear. The drops from the spear, when they pulled it free, coagulated and formed the continents. After this, the first kami and human beings were created. When Izanami died in childbirth, Izanagi tried to retrieve her from the underworld. However, he was unable to do so and was polluted by his journey. When he returned, he cleansed himself in the River of Tachibana, thus beginning the ritual practice of misogi. Literal translation, "He Who Invites" and "She Who Invites."

Kamidana A household altar for enshrinement of kami.

Kandakara Treasures brought by the kami.

Kannagara The way of nature, the ceaseless ebb and flow of the universe.

Kegare Impurities, pollution of one's self or other individuals; the exhausting of life vitality. May be removed by *harai* to restore original purity.

Kotodama Literally, "word soul." Refers to the sacred vibrational quality of a sound and/or a word.

Kunitsu Kami Earthly Kami.

Makoto Honesty, truthfulness, conscientiousness.

Matsuri (奉) or matsuru To revere the kami, to conduct ritual to venerate the divine spirit; to present offerings with humility, gratitude and appreciation; to humbly perform a service for others. (Not to be confused with "matsuri" 祭 festival)

Misogi Ritual purification in cold water, as in a waterfall, river, or ocean.

Mitama The divided spirit of kami. This allows the essence or spirit of the kami to be in multiple locations simultaneously, just as fire can be divided without lessening the intensity of the original flame.

Nirei nihakushu ippai Two bows, two claps, one bow.

Norito Words addressed to kami, recited in ancient style of language with emphasis on *kotodama*. Generally includes words of praise for the kami, lists of offerings, words identifying persons pronouncing the prayer, and the subject of the prayer.

Ofuda Tablet on which the name of a kami is written. May be enshrined in *kamidana* or placed in home or other building.

Oshiki Wooden tray on which offerings to kami are placed.

Saishu The main officient in a ceremony; either a priest or priestess.

Sanbo Wooden stand on which offerings to kami are placed.

Sarutahiko no Ō Kami Head of the Earthly Kami and kami of guidance and protection. Husband of Ame no Uzume no Mikoto. Enshrined at Tsubaki Ō Kami Yashiro.

Seiza Sitting position: kneeling, with knees bent and legs folded under the body.

Shide Strips of cloth or paper folded in a zigzag, spiraling shape; symbolic of spiral energy connecting Heaven and Earth.

Shinsen Food offerings presented to kami. May include rice, sake, rice cakes, fish, fowl, meat, seaweed, vegetables, fruits, sweets, salt, and water.

Shubatsu Purification performed before a ceremony or rite.

Takama no Hara High Expanse of Heaven.

Tama Spirit, soul.

Tamagushi Offering to kami of evergreen branch with *shide* attached.

Te Mizu Use of water to purify hands and mouth before worshipping at a shrine.

Tsubaki Ō Kami Yashiro Tsubaki Grand Shrine located near Suzuka City, Mie Prefecture, Japan. Primary shrine of Sarutahiko no Ō Kami and Ame no Uzume no Mikoto. Founded in 3 B.C.

Tsumi Impurities and impediments between one's self and other people or between one's self and the environment that may be removed by purification, or *harai*.

Ubusuna no Ō Kami One's guardian kami, often the kami of one's birthplace.

Yaoyorozu no Ō Kami Myriad of kami who support the Earthly Kami and Heavenly Kami.

APPENDIX C

SHRINE ETIQUETTE

Te Mizu (Hand Purification)

When visiting a shrine, it is customary to purify one's self before approaching the kami by washing your hands (*te mizu*).

Temizuya
Tsubaki Grand Shrine of America
Granite Falls, Washington

A water basin will be located at the entrance to the shrine.

(1) With the ladle in your right hand, rinse your left hand; (the rinse water should spill onto the gravel, not back into the basin)

(2) holding the ladle in your left hand, rinse your right hand;

(3) hold the ladle in your right hand, pouring water into your left cupped hand, and rinse out your mouth, spitting out the water onto the rock area outside the basin

(4) rinse your left hand again, and then

(5) empty the remaining water in the ladle by letting the water pour vertically down the handle, cleansing the handle for the next person.

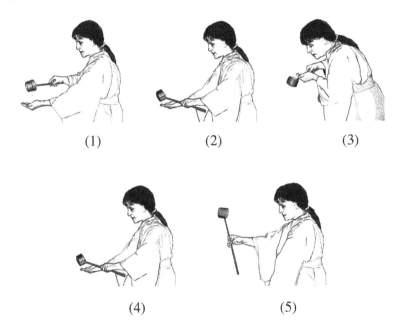

(1)   (2)   (3)

(4)   (5)

Matsuri: Offerings

Next, it is customary to make an offering by dropping money into the *saisen bako*, or wooden offering box in front of the shrine.

You then would present your prayers to the kami and perform *nirei nihakushu ippai* as described in the section below.

If you request a special ceremony to be performed on your behalf, it is customary to make an additional offering called *hatsuhoryo* in gratitude for the services of the shrine and the protection of the kami.

The term *matsuri* (also pronounced *tatematsuru*) refers not only to offerings, but describes a state of mind—of reverence and gratitude that encompasses the act of making an offering to the kami. There is no specific time during a ceremony when offerings will be requested; rather, it is up to the individual to present offerings to the kami and for the support of the shrine.

Offerings of other types may also be presented to the kami, including sake, salt, fresh fruits and vegetables, and other gifts given from the heart and with gratitude.

Nirei Nihakushu Ippai (2 Bows, 2 Claps, 1 Bow)

When entering the shrine, announce your presence to the kami by performing *nirei nihakushu ippai* (two claps, two bows, one clap).

When bowing, bend approximately 90 degrees, showing respect for the kami and with a feeling of humility and gratitude.

When clapping, the hands are held at chest height in front of the body with the palms facing each other. Slide the right hand back slightly so that the fingertips of your right hand are about 1 inch back. With the hands slightly cupped, clap twice, making a sharp sound. This sound helps purify the environment of any stagnant or negative energy. In addition, the initial clap is a sending of energy outward, while the second clap is a receiving of energy. In this way, you are acknowledging the flow of nature, the *in/yo* (yin/yang) duality of existence, and the importance of giving as well as receiving.

The final bow is a "closing" of this ritual, with a feeling of gratitude for the gifts of life you receive.

Shubatsu (Purification)

When a priest performs *shubatsu*, he is purifying the participants by waving a *haraigushi*, a branch or wooden pole with *shide*, or folded paper spirals. The symbolism of this action is the "sweeping away" of impurities. One should bow slightly (45 degrees) during purification.

Tamagushi (Offering Branch)

The *tamagushi* offering is a ritual of presenting an evergreen branch with a *shide* (folded paper spiral) attached.

The evergreen branch is symbolic of the longevity and gift of life. In Japan they use *sakaki* branches, a plant that is native to Japan, but not usually available in North America. As an alternative, you may use a similar plant that has dark green leaves and flat branches.

The *shide* is made of folded paper. The spiral shape is symbolic of the divine energy that spirals down from Heaven and up from Earth.

The original Shinto shrines in ancient days were sacred groves of trees. Sacred prayers were chanted by the *kannushi*, or priest, entreating the kami to descend to the sacred location. The tall, vertical trees, were the spires upon which the kami would alight.

Thus, the use of evergreen branches connects us to this ancient ritual.

When handed a tamagushi,

(1) place your right hand on top of the stem, holding the branch end from below with your left hand.

(2) slide your left hand down to the stem, moving your right hand behind the leafy portion. Pause, with the branch held in front of you, giving thanks to the kami for your blessings and spiritually "placing" your prayer request in the branch.

(3) lowering the branch, turn it clockwise, with the stem pointing toward the kami, and place the branch on the table.

(4) bow twice, clap twice, bow once.

(6) take a small step back, making a slight bow, indicating completion of your ritual.

(7) step off the center line, and make a slight bow toward *saishu* (the priest leading the ceremony)

To prepare *tamagushi* for offering in your own ceremony, make a small *shide* from white paper (preferably rice paper or a similar soft paper) as shown below:

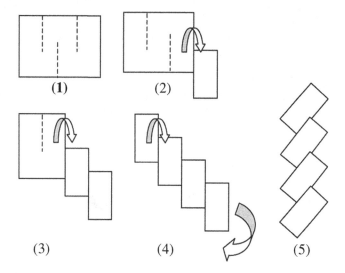

Shide may also be hung to indicate a sacred location or natural formation (such as a tree, rock, waterfall).

Conclusion of Ceremony

At the conclusion of the ceremony, it is customary to bow and thank *saishu* for conducting the ceremony. The polite phrase in Japanese for "thank you" is *"Dōmo arigato gozaimasu."*

After the ceremony, you will be offered a shallow cup (*kawarake*) of sacred rice wine, or *o-miki*. This is an honor to drink wine whose essence has been blessed and shared with the kami. Holding the cup with both hands, drink the sake in three sips. Then, replace the cup on the tray, take a small step back, and bow slightly in gratitude.

Leaving the Shrine

Just before leaving the shrine, bow slightly toward the altar before leaving the room. This is a custom for departing with gratitude and humility.

APPENDIX D

KAMIDANA

Kamidana literally means "kami shelf." This is the term used for a miniature shrine that is placed in the home on a shelf.

When choosing a space for your *kamidana*, place it in an area that can be a sacred space, where you can pause for prayer and reflection. This may be a shelf in a library or den, or it may be in a corner of your living room or kitchen. Wherever it is placed, the immediate area becomes sacred and should be treated respectfully.

Having a *kamidana* in your home is a reminder to begin each day with gratitude and with prayer and to close your day in the same manner. It also creates a site where the *mitama*, or divided spirit, of the kami will reside, bringing energy from the divine into your home. It is here that you will seek guidance, protection, and harmony from the divine spiritual beings—the kami.

Traditionally, a *kamidana* is a miniature shrine and may be purchased from a Shinto shrine. *Ofuda*, a paper tablet with the name of the kami inscribed on it, is placed inside the *kamidana*. The kami is called upon to descend in spirit, and the kami's essence reside in the *Ofuda*.

In front of the shrine, symbolic offerings to the kami are placed:

Rice	米
Water	水
Salt	塩
Sake	酒
Evergreen branches	榊

The placement of the offerings differs, depending on whether they are offered on a tray or whether they are lined up (see below):

sake sake
rice
water salt

water sake rice salt

125

APPENDIX E

MISOGI

Misogi is a ritual of physically cleansing one's body and spirit in cold water. This is traditionally done in a river, waterfall, or the ocean.

The practice originates from the mythology recorded in the *Kojiki* where Izanagi, after visiting the "bottom country," or place of afterlife, returned to Earth and ritually bathed in the Tachibana River to rid himself of impurities.

After ritually purifying one's self, the impurities are carried down the rivers by the kami Seoritsu Hime to the ocean. Where the river meets the sea, Hayakitsu Hime swallows the impurities and carries them to the bottom country, where Ibukido Nushi expels them. Haya Sasura Meto then seizes and dissolves the impurities, ridding us of imperfection and returning us to our pristine, natural state.

Through the purification practice, or *gyo*, of misogi we thus aim to purify and intensify our *tamashii*, or soul. Guji Yukitaka Yamamoto writes,

> Misogi is effective in restoring the natural greatness of soul of which man is capable. Misogi in the style of Tsubaki Grand Shrine has been practiced for centuries, and there is good reason to believe that people in ages

past knew more of the secrets of nature than we know in our modern state of alienation from nature. My own experience with misogi for almost 60 years convinces me of its power to do many good things for those who are receptive to its healing and renewing power.[1]

Those taking part in misogi change into clothing for the ritual. Men wear white loincloths called *funodoshi*, and women wear white, kimono-like robes called *mizugoromo*. Both wear head bands called *hachimaki*.

Next, participants assemble in the shrine to recite "Misogi Ō Harai" and to receive a simplified form of *Ō Harai* called *shubatsu*. Since the waterfall, river, or ocean is itself a kami, there is a need for purification before entering.

---

[1] Yukitaka Yamamoto, Kami no Michi: The Way of the Kami (Stockton, Calif.: Tsubaki America, 1999), p. 117.

After arriving at the misogi area, we face the main shrine and perform *nirei nihakushu ippai* (2 bows, 2 claps, 1 bow) toward the kami.

Next we commence warm-up movements to prepare ourselves physically, mentally, and spiritually for misogi.

The sequence of practice is outlined as follows:

1. Furitama (soul shaking)

- Chant "Harae do no Ō Kami"
- Hands are cupped together, with the right hand on top, with a space the size of an egg in between
- The hands gently move vertically in front of the lower abdomen to invigorate tamashii

Furitama entreats the kami of the place of *harai* to be present for purification ritual. Shaking the *tama* or soul stimulates awareness and *ki*, or life energy.

2. Torifune (bird rowing)

- 1st sequence: left leg forward; shout "yi-e" in rhythm to rowing; clench fists with thumbs inside; lean forward and move arms as though rowing a boat. 20 Repetitions. Furitama.
- 2nd sequence: right leg forward; shout "ei-ho." 20 repetitions. Furitama.
- 3rd sequence: left leg forward; shout "yie-sa." 20 repetitions. Furitama.

Torifune readies the physical body for the austere practice of misogi.

3. Otakebi (shouting)

- Following *michihiko* (leader), stand with hands on hips, feet apart, shouting the following chants:
    - Iku tama!
    - Taru tama!
    - Tama tamaru tama!
- Following *michihiko*, repeat the following chant 3 times:
    - Ō Kami! Ō Kami!
    - Kunitsu Ō Kami!
    - Sarutahiko no Ō Kami tōtoshiya!

Otakebi is a series of chants that activate the soul, affirm the awareness of the infinite in your soul, and invoke Sarutahiko no Ō Kami, head of all Earthly kami, to be present.

4. Okorobi (yielding)

- Stand with left hand on hip, feet apart, right hand with 2 fingers extended as a sword, held to forehead
- Shout the name of each of the following kami, vigorously cutting the air after each name while shouting "yi-e" sharply (referred to as "*toin.*" As you cut the air, take a step forward with your left foot and then back again.
    - Kuni Toko Tachi no Mikoto! (yi-e)
    - Sarutahiko no Ō Kami! (yi-e)
    - Kokuryu no Ō Kami (yi-e)

Okorobi invokes 3 important kami: Kuni Toko Tachi no Miikoto, Earthly kami of vertical energy; Sarutahiko no Ō Kami, head of all Earthly kami and kami of guidance; and Kokuryu no Ō Kami, the kami of water, life, and ki.

5. Ibuki undo (breathing)

- Stand with feet apart.
- Lower your hands to "scoop" the energy of the Earth in an outward motion.
- Raise your hands toward Heaven, "scooping" the Heavenly energy and bringing your hands together in a cupped manner.
- Lower your hands toward your hara (approximately 2 inches below navel), ending with a slight shaking motion to transfer the energy to your tama.
- Repeat 5 times.

Ibuki is a practice for receiving the ki of the universe.

6. Nyusui (entering the water)

- Face toward the water, performing furitama (step 1) while *michihiko* prepares for misogi.
- *Michihiko* will spray sake and salt into the misogi area, sprinkle purifying salt on you, recite Kujihō Norito, and cut away impurities by performing *toin*.
- When it is your turn to enter the water, follow these steps (note that when performing misogi in a waterfall, participants enter one by one; if performing misogi in a river, lake, or ocean all participants will enter together):
- Clap your hands twice; bow once (toward the water)
- Perform *toin* (cutting air, shouting "yi-e.")
- Clasp your hands in front of you, with middle fingers extended

- Enter the water, repeating the following chant until *michihiko* signals you to come out of the water (men turn counter-clockwise when entering water, women turn clockwise):

  Harae tamai
  Kiyome tamai
  Rokkonshōjō

- After coming out of the water, again repeat *toin*, clap twice, bow toward the water
- Bow slightly to *michihiko*
- Face shrine and perform *nirei nihakushu ippai*

In discussing misogi, Guji Yamamoto writes:

In Shinto the *gyo*[2] is misogi, purification under a waterfall, a part of our practices at Tsubaki Grand Shrine. Misogi is demanding, and many people feel uncertain or even afraid of standing under the waterfall. Yet our *Misogi-kai*, misogi association, has a large membership of regular participants from all walks of life who seek something more spiritual in life amid the materialism and indifference they find in everyday life.

In Shinto misogi is the primary act that can produce purification and enhance the spirituality of those who practice it. As human beings we are the children of the kami and as such we try to work for the progress of human culture. The shrine is a place where human beings and the kami may meet and be united. Misogi is one of the ways in which that meeting can be effected.

---

[2] Gyo refers to a discipline or practice.

In Shinto belief, human beings can come close to the kami through training and discipline. The human soul inclines naturally toward the kami and can be cultivated to become more deeply related through the right kind of activities. This is a matter for attention every day.[3]

People seeking to be close to the kami should work at showing cleanliness, brightness and diligence in all they do and should seek to cultivate harmony in personal relations. Misogi regularly practiced can help one achieve this.

---

[3] *Kami no Michi: The Way of the Kami*, p. 116.

APPENDIX F

CHINKON

Chinkon gyōhō is a sacred spiritual practice for reviving the energy of the soul, for reactivating and intensifying spiritual energy. It is also referred to as *tama furi*, which is shaking, stirring, or vibrating the soul.

Although the ancient origins of Chinkon gyōhō are uncertain, this practice has been taught at Iso no Kami Shrine since the 4th century. Guji Masamitsu Mori, Chief Priest of Iso no Kami Jingu, teaches that chinkon is a method to revive the original power of the human being.

Practiced on a regular basis, chinkon will enliven the sacred power that resides within you. It is said that even if you are dead, you can return to life again through this sacred chanting.[1]

Chinkon gyōhō should be performed in a quiet place, preferably with dim light and candles. The initial section of the practice consists of various prayers and chants. The second section consists of chanting and motions; movements in this part are vigorous in order to stir and enliven the spirit. The third section also consists of chanting and motions, but is performed in a more calm manner, allowing the invigorated spirit to resettle, now intensified.

---

[1] Rev. Masamitsu Mori. Interview with author March 1, 2001.

The fourth and fifth sections consist of breathing meditation and prayers.

Chinkon gyōhō is a mystical practice. It is best taught by an experienced practitioner in order to understand the subtle nuances and correct technique. However, hereafter follows a brief outline as a reference for Shinto followers who wish to broaden their practice.

Chinkon Gyōhō

Preliminary Meditation:

Sitting position: seiza
Hand position: clasped, right on top, with egg-size cavity in between. Gently shake clasped hands in vertical motion

Furitama: chant "Sarutahiko no Ō Kami"

Section 1

Sitting position: seiza
Hand position: palms together flat, held in front in prayer

Recitations:
Ō Harahi no Kotoba
Tokusa no Harae no Kotoba

Hi Fu Mi Norito (5 times)

Mikusa no Ō Harahi (5 times)

Tokusa no Kandakara (5 times)

(the last line "Furube yura yura to furube" is only recited on the final repetition)

Nirei Nihakushu Ippai (2 Bows, 2 Claps, 1 Bow)

Silent Meditation

Ippai (1 Bow)

Section 2

Sitting position: legs bent, soles of feet together

Hand position: changes with each recitation; between positions, do not part the hands. Continue to protect the energy within.

Furitama; silently chant "Sarutahiko no O Kami" while shaking hands gently, as performed during preliminary meditation. Note that the left hand is on top here.

<u>Recitations:</u>

Hi Fu Mi Norito (hands clasped in front at chest level, left hand on top; rotate slowly until right hand on top)

Kandakara (hands clasped with fingers in-
terlaced, left thumb on top, in front at chest
level; after chant, bring clasped hands to level
of tama, or just below navel)

Hi Fu Mi Yo I Mu Na Ya Ko To (3 times, with the motion
sequence below. Make one circular motion for each syllable
chanted)

- Left knee, counter-clockwise
- Right knee, clockwise
- Front, down, up, and in
- Front, up, down, and in
- Vertically

Kandakara (hold hands clasped in front at chest level. At end of
norito, open hands facing upward to return kandakara to the
kami with spiritual appreciation)

Section 3

Sitting position: legs bent, soles of feet together
Hand position: clasped with index fingers
together, pointing to heaven; left thumb on top
of right thumb

Recitation:

Hi Fu Mi Yo I Mu Na Ya Ko To (3 times, with motion sequence below. Chant entire sequence with each motion)

- Vertically, up and down once
- Left knee, counter-clockwise
- Right knee, clockwise
- Front, down, up, and in
- Front, up, down, and in
- Front, counter-clockwise
- Front, clockwise
- Vertically, up and down once

Section 4

Sitting position: legs bent, soles of feet together
Hand position: same as prior section

Ibuki Undo (Breathing)
10 cycles. Each cycle: breathe in 10 seconds through nose; breathe out 20 seconds through mouth.

Section 5

Sitting position: seiza

Ippai (one deep bow)
Silent meditation
Nirei (two bows)

<u>Recitations:</u>
(hand position: palms flat together, in prayer)
Shin Paishi
Tatae Goto
Goshu no Shinka

Nirei Nihakushu Ippai (2 Bows, 2 Claps, 1 Bow)

Printed in the United States
By Bookmasters